'Frank Paul is a dazzling quizzer.'

VICTORIA COREN MITCHELL

'The sultan of spoonerisms and the Aga Khan of anagrams.'

ALEX BELLOS, GUARDIAN

'There is no other book, to my knowledge, like this one. It is weird and wonderful, bizarre and challenging and thrilling... Frank Paul has created something that defies pigeon-holing... one of the most rewarding books that you could read this year... a quiz book to cherish.'

GARETH KINGSTON, ALL THINGS QUIZ

'I urge you to enter Frank Paul's world, a more beautiful version of our own.'

ALAN CONNOR, AUTHOR OF THE JOY OF QUIZ

'Frank Paul's quizzes are always a devious, diverting delight. This is his magnum opus, a fascinating web of trickery, trivia, high and low culture woven with verve and wit.'

STUART MACONIE

'It's like a brilliant escape room had a baby with a cryptic crossword.'

DARRAGH ENNIS, THE CHASE

'Twelve tales of charming complexity.'

HUGH STEPHENSON, GUARDIAN CROSSWORD EDITOR

'The love child of Only Connect and Mastermind, born in Discworld.'

LISA THIEL, EGGHEAD

'It's brilliant. There is no more perfect book for the more discerning quizzer.'

EMMA KENNEDY

'I've no idea what is going on in the world that is Frank Paul's brain. But I do enjoy holidaying there.'

JOHN HENDERSON, ALIAS ENIGMATIST

**FRANK PAUL** is a fine artist and a superstar in the world of quizzes. He is the author of *The Cryptic Pub Quiz*. An *Only Connect* champion, he also served as a Trapper on *The Answer Trap*. He lives in Cambridge where he runs The Mill pub quiz.

# THE TWELVE
# QUIZZES
# OF CHRISTMAS

## FRANK PAUL

ONEWORLD

A Oneworld Book

First published by Oneworld Publications in 2022
This paperback edition published 2023

ISBN 978-0-86154-681-7
eISBN 978-0-86154-397-7

Typeset by Tetragon, London
Printed and bound in Great Britain by Clays Ltd, Elcograf S.p.A.

Oneworld Publications
10 Bloomsbury Street
London WC1B 3SR
England

Stay up to date with the latest books,
special offers, and exclusive content from
Oneworld with our newsletter

Sign up on our website
oneworld-publications.com

*In memory of Steve*

# TABLE OF CONTENTS

# SCORECARD

| SCORE FOR THIS ROUND (PLAYER/TEAM 1) | TOTAL SCORE SO FAR (PLAYER/TEAM 1) | SCORE FOR THIS ROUND (PLAYER/TEAM 2) | TOTAL SCORE SO FAR (PLAYER/TEAM 2) |
| --- | --- | --- | --- |
| | | | |
| | | | |
| | | | |
| | | | |
| | | | |
| | | | |
| | | | |
| | | | |
| | | | |
| | | | |
| | | | |
| | | | |
| | | | |
| | | | |
| | | | |
| | | | |
| | | | |
| | | | |
| | | | |
| | | | |
| | | | |
| | | | |
| | | | |
| | | | |
| | | | |
| | | | |
| | | | |
| | | | |
| | | | |
| | | | |
| | | | |
| | | | |
| | | | |
| | | | |

# PREFACE

I very much hope you enjoy this book! I realize it's rather fiendish at times. Here are six things to bear in mind as you play:

1. Keep a written record of your answers! You may need to re-examine them when solving later puzzles.

2. Do use the hints provided when you need to! They still leave you with quite a bit of puzzling to do, hopefully accompanied by a sense of satisfaction once the puzzle is finished. Attempting to complete the book without them is the equivalent of playing a video game on the hardest difficulty setting.

3. The answers to rounds of questions are often interlinked, and may be linked to the answers in other rounds of the same quiz, so don't despair if you can't figure an answer out, as you might be able to piece it together from clues hidden elsewhere.

4. If you haven't solved enough of the 'ordinary' questions to decode a puzzle question, you may look up the answers to the 'ordinary' questions before attempting the puzzle. Obviously, you may not earn points for the questions whose answers you've looked up, but you may still earn points for the puzzle.

5. You may find it rewarding to play the quizzes in this book as part of a team. The puzzles are multilayered and the questions often require diverse knowledge, which is well suited to a group all chipping in with ideas.

6. Some puzzles involve grids, as well as other things intended to be drawn on. If you baulk at the idea of drawing on a book, consider making copies of the relevant pages.

# IT'S A WONDERFUL MULTIVERSE

*Hint on page 201*

*Answers on page 219*

You are a woman named Infinity Quincunx. Your home town has been lawless and depraved for as long as you can remember. Today you compete in the trivia night at the Satan Crater. The host asks:

1. We all love a nice, juicy human sacrifice! Amrish, whose character practises human sacrifice in *Indiana Jones and the Temple of Doom*, shared what surname with Om, who starred in *East Is East*? It's also the name of an Indian snack consisting of deep-fried dough.

2. A film, where Johnny Galecki's character is among those murdered by a mysterious hook-wielding figure, and from three years later a hit song, whose singer claims, 'I'm not that innocent', share which antepenultimate word in their titles?

3. The surname of the first woman to run the Boston Marathon as a registered entrant (who was notoriously attacked by an official while participating); a red Teletubby with a circle at the tip of her antenna; a substance which may be slang for 'kill' or 'diamonds'; and any one of various appendages a fish uses for swimming and balance: which four-letter word, if added to the end of each of these, makes them have something in common?

4. Which word, the title of Ed Sheeran's first UK number one single, is repeated in the name of a prison in which Julius and Ethel Rosenberg were executed?

5. A man associated with a classic Christmas song gave this (probably false) account of how he earned his nickname:

3

'I would haul out my trusty six-shooters, made of wood, and loudly exclaim, "_____! _____!" As my luckless victim fell clutching his side, I would shout, "_____! _____!", and I would let him have it again.' Which word fills these blank spaces?

6. Which word for a loud, low sound, when written once, is the title of an Anastacia song, when written twice is the title of a John Lee Hooker song, when written three times is the title of an Outhere Brothers song and when written four times is the title of a Vengaboys song?

7. Meanings of which word, which is spelt identically to a previous answer except for the insertion of an extra letter, include an alcoholic drink and a weapon used to lethal effect by a biblical character?

8. By what five-letter name is the American company with the motto 'Arms Makers for Responsible Citizens' commonly known? It may be preceded by one letter to make the surname of a psychologist known for collaborating with David Dunning.

The questions are worth one point each (as are all the questions in this book unless otherwise indicated). The scores are announced. Your competitors have cheated relentlessly and you finish last. Cannibal Helen, naked except for a greasy apron adorned with lewd doodles, marches slowly towards you, drool trickling from her leering lips. Every week she eats the loser with apricot chutney.

But a man has scrambled to the stage. He is tall and gangly. He looks desperately at the crowd.

'Don't you know me? I'm your old pal Jim!'

There are murmurs of confusion. Jim starts pointing at the crowd and yelling that instead of stranglers and cannibals, they're all housewives and Sunday school teachers.

While the crowd jeer at Jim, you sneak out. Snow whirls in the bitter wind. But there's nowhere you can go where Helen won't find you. You lurch across the icy roads to the bridge. Far below, the river froths round the rocks. You lean over the railing, wondering how it will feel to hit the water.

Then you hear a voice. It's a distant, frail voice but with a strange power to it. The wind's howl seems to die down to let it be heard.

'Infinity Quincunx jumps to her death now.'

You look back. Through the snow you spot a small man, huddled in an oversized coat, his white hair glistening beneath a fedora, shuffling on the other side of the road. And there's Jim walking next to him! Jim is agitated, striding back and forth and waving his arms.

'No! No!' Jim protests.

The little white-haired man lays a hand on his back and guides him on.

'Hey!' you yell. You run after the pair, who don't seem to hear. '*Hey!*' you screech again.

They turn.

'Infinity?' says Jim. 'You didn't jump! Oh, thank goodness you're alive!'

The little man is flustered. 'What do you mean by not jumping? You were supposed to die – I had it figured out!'

'I was going to, then I heard your voice. . .' you say.

'Oh, bother, bother, bother!' mutters the little man. 'My silly old voice!'

'But this is wonderful, Milbert!' gushes Jim. 'She was supposed to die but she didn't!'

'It is *not* wonderful!' snaps Milbert. 'Nothing in this world is wonderful! Helen will eat her anyway. Come on.'

He tugs Jim's sleeve and they *vanish* into thin air. Not even a puff of smoke!

You've got to find Jim and Milbert. Milbert seems powerful, even *magical*. OK, he does seem to want you dead, but maybe you can persuade him to save you? You stagger on through the storm, through street after street, hoping Helen won't find you before you find them. Is that them in the town square, deep in the distance? Yes, yes, Jim is on his knees now. 'Please. . . get me home. .'

Helen bounds from a doorway, gnawing a greasy bone and cradling an axe. 'You're mine, Quincunx!' she slavers.

You run full-pelt for Milbert and Jim. Milbert clasps his hands as if in prayer. He opens them up and dazzling lights beam from his palms. Jim clutches Milbert's wrists. Milbert finally notices you and gives you an infuriated look.

'Please go away, Miss Quincunx, this is the climax.'

You hear footsteps crunching towards you. You shove Jim aside, sending him sprawling to the snow. You seize Milbert by the shoulders. 'Listen to me. . .' you begin, but your voice is sucked away as light engulfs you.

The light fades.

'Am I. . . dead?' you ask.

'No, and stop reminding me of it!' exclaims Milbert. 'Oh, this is awful!'

Jim and Helen are gone. You're still in the town square. . . or are you? It looks immaculately festive. A glittering Christmas tree towers before you.

'Where am I?'

'Reality!'

'*Reality?* Then where was I before?'

'In a world I created. I forged it, and all your memories, out of the worst path every one of you could have taken if you'd followed your basest desires. I got the idea soon after they made me Jim's guardian angel. You see, Jim was in the depths of despair. He wished he'd never been born. I showed him your world – a world without him, a world of sin – to teach him the value of his life. Helen's nasty eating habits, Julian losing his favourite hat, your suicide – all these were meant to shock him to his senses. But just as I was about to bring him back to reality, you shoved him aside and took his place! You abandoned him in your fake world, which closed around him as soon as I left! And I can't go back there – only angels with wings can enter locked dimensions!'

'My death isn't any more shocking than Julian losing a hat?'

'You're a peripheral character, Infinity Quincunx! Oh, I'll never get my wings now! We angels are supposed to earn them, but it's taking me *centuries.*'

'I need a drink.'

You head for the Satan Crater, with Milbert following behind and murmuring wretchedly.

6

But now it's not the Satan Crater but the Prudent Clergyman.

'Time for trivia, everybody!' coos the quiz host. 'Please get your pencils out. Be sure they're not too sharp: we don't want anybody getting hurt. Let's start with a nice pious question.' A round of applause greets this announcement.

1.  The theologian J. I. Packer wrote, 'The _____ ethic of nurture was to train up children in the way they should go, to care for their bodies and souls together, and to educate them for sober, godly, socially useful adult living.' Which seven-letter word, relating to a Protestant group, fills the blank space? It is an anagram of two consecutive words found within Packer's quotation.

2.  Another theologian, C. S. Lewis, wrote, 'We are told that Christ was killed for us, that His death has washed out our sins, and that by dying He _____ death itself.' The Reverend Jesse Jackson once said, 'The white, the Hispanic, the black, the Arab, the Jew, the woman, the native American, the small farmer, the businessperson, the environmentalist, the peace activist, the young, the old, the lesbian, the gay, and the _____ make up the American quilt.' Which word, which begins and ends with the same letter, fills both blank spaces?

3.  Suaasat, a soup often made with seal meat, is a traditional dish of which large island? A species of shark named after this island is thought to be Earth's longest-living vertebrate.

4.  Which word is shared in the title of a *Carry On* film parodying Hammer horror films and the stage name of a musician who founded the Official Monster Raving Loony Party?

5.  A tee, a trap and an elbow are among the items used in what? This word is ultimately derived from a Latin word for lead (the metal).

6.  Which emotion was the subject of a namesake documentary by Canadian filmmaker Albert Nerenberg, who describes the emotion as 'one of the key factors in relapse with people that have addictions'? The documentary

inspired an awards ceremony, which named then-Prime Minster Stephen Harper as the Canadian most likely to engender this emotion. The word I'm looking for can be pluralized to make the name of an experimental Japanese band.

7. Which word meaning 'asleep' fills the blank space in this extract from the song 'My Grandfather's Clock'?

> Ninety years without \_\_\_\_\_,
> (Tick, tick, tick, tick,)
> His life seconds numbering,
> (Tick, tick, tick, tick,)
> It stopped short,
> Never to go again,
> When the old man died.

8. Finally, I'm proud to say that every one of us in this town is a stickler for regulations. Which word meaning 'stickler for regulations' is an anagram of 'leg mourner'?

You hand in your sheet and head for the bar. You order a whisky.

'This is a respectable establishment!' shrieks the barmaid. 'Alcohol is Satan's dribble!'

It takes you a second to realize, but the barmaid is. . . Helen. You barely recognized her in her long grey dress and pearl necklace, her sleek hair gathered in a bun.

'Don't you get all preachy when you're a cannibal!' you yell.

The Prudent Clergyman's clientele gasp in unison. Then they turn on you, shouting, 'Bearer of false witness!' and 'Venomous Jezebel!'

You scream back, accusing them of all the crimes and debaucheries they committed in your world.

'It's so dreadfully upsetting!' weeps Helen. 'I've never been treated so viciously.'

A woman rushes to comfort her. Helen's weeping turns to a feral snarl as she sinks her teeth into the woman's arm. It takes ten of the bar's clients to wrestle her away.

'It's true!' Helen proclaims, her eyes gleaming wide, a torrent of blood surging from her maw. 'I've always wanted to do that and it was more glorious than I'd ever imagined! When my secret was exposed, I realized there was no sense in restraining myself any longer!'

The other clients start declaring that they've always wanted to commit the transgressions you accused them of.

'And I've always wanted to punch somebody!' yells Fred McCorkenstrum, whom you've only ever known as a quiet man who collected stamps. He thumps the man next to him. A mass brawl breaks out.

Once again you sneak out of the bar. Milbert follows.

'We've corrupted the entire town!' he wails. 'I'll never be able to show my face in Heaven again! The only way I can possibly redeem myself is by doing the dozen!'

'What's doing the dozen?'

'The pinnacle of achievement for any Christmas angel. You know how I described this world as "reality"? Well, it's one of many realities, and doing the dozen means bringing Christmas happy endings to *twelve* of them. It's barely possible! Angels have been reduced to blubbering buffoons trying! But we have to try – it's the only chance I have of earning my wings and breaking Jim free! I'll need your help, Miss Quincunx. There'll be questions and puzzles to solve. We angels aren't supposed to meddle in such things, so you'll have to do it for me. I'll be beside you, but invisible, intangible and only faintly smellable. I'll appear if you call on me for help – you'll be docked points for it, though. Keep track of your points. In each dimension, you'll be at the heart of a new Christmas tale. You may be plunged into a whole new body. To start the quest, I must summon up eight differently coloured lights from the palms of my hands. They're supposed to be colours that first were absent but later appeared.

'What might they be, Miss Quincunx?'

You recall the answers from the two trivia nights. Inspiration dawns.

**What are the eight colours?**

(This question, being written in bold, is a puzzle question. As indicated by the symbol on the right, it is worth two points if answered without Milbert's help, and one point if you consult him via the 'Hints' section.)

# WINTERLUDE 1

*Answers on page 220*

You and Milbert are whisked away. You feel like you are on a rollercoaster with kaleidoscopes glued to your eyes, rocketing through a hall of mirrors in the midst of a tornado. Milbert turns towards you, his face bursting into fragments and reassembling itself every fraction of a second, while a galaxy of glittering reflections reels around him.

'You are pale, Miss Quincunx,' says Milbert, sounding like a thousand Milberts speaking slightly out of sync. 'You'll need your strength and your spirits if we're to have any hope of saving Jim. Look, I have some Christmas crackers here, a joke in every one. Have you heard, "My wife's gone to the West Indies. Jamaica? No, she wanted to go"? It's rather amusing, don't you think? These jokes are like that – but you supply the place name.'

1. My husband's gone to West London.
   
   _____?
   
   No, it's constructed largely from bricks and other building materials.

2. My wife's going to the Republic of China to give a blood transfusion.
   
   _____?
   
   No, O-negative.

3. My husband's going to India to see a concert by the singer who released 'Love Me Like You Do'.
   
   _____?
   
   No, I expect her to be fully clothed.

4. I'm going to take the presenter of *That's Life* to Hampshire.

    _____?

    No, I'll transport her in a car.

5. I'm going to Germany to address the former lead singer of The Birthday Party in a cat-like voice.

    _____?

    Yes, that's exactly what I plan to do.

6. Tipper Gore's gone to a city in North Africa.

    _____?

    No, his relationship to her is friendly rather than mocking.

7. Hello, dear friend who pronounces every second word with a lisp, my wife's going to Merseyside to watch pigs play badminton.

    _____?

    No, the activity's open to pigs of any gender.

You have grown so absorbed in filling in the blank spaces that you don't notice the world around you slowing, growing dimmer. You become aware that you are in a cold room and a thin sheet is draped over you. You reach out to pull the sheet up, but jump back at the sight of your withered hands, translucent skin stretched over thick veins and rugged knuckles.

# A CHRISTMAS KRILL

*Hints on page* 201

*Answers on page* 221

*In this quiz, where an item is underlined, you may take it with you as you travel through time.*

You are wearing a woollen dress over your nightgown. The wind rattles the windows. In the middle of the room a speck of white light appears, expanding and growing more dazzling. It subsides to reveal a pale young girl in a wide, frilly dress, from whom an ethereal glow radiates.

'Genevieve Krill,' she intones blankly, her voice shrill and eerie. 'Your heart is filled with anger.'

She extends a tiny hand. Unthinkingly you reach for it. An intense, dizzying sensation fills your head and you clamp your eyes shut.

You open your eyes to find yourself behind a pillar in a hall. 'This is where your bitterness begins,' whispers the spectral girl. You peep out to see three bemused dogs perching by <u>photographs of celebrities</u>. An elderly man and a young woman enter; he unlocks a box labelled 'Which dog should win?' while she watches, shifting from foot to foot.

The man withdraws a piece of paper from the box. *Genevieve Krill's dog is the winner and the others are drooling prats*, he reads with furrowed brow. 'But this is a forgery, Miss Krill; I know Mr Clogitt's handwriting as well as any man. Besides, you left this <u>envelope</u> behind, headed, "Mind-bending master plan", containing your plan to forge a note purportedly from Mr Clogitt if he does not turn up. Disappointing behaviour, even by your standards.

As Mr Clogitt, being the only judge, has not submitted a slip of paper, I declare the contest not only null but also, I'm afraid, void.'

'This is ludicrous!' yells the young woman. 'My dog's a dead ringer for Adam West – the way he sits, his resolute gaze ahead like he's just brought the Joker to justice. Those other two wretched mutts look like they've entered a contest to see who *least* resembles Audrey Hepburn and Althea Gibson! I demand to be named the winner! What happened to Clogitt – why isn't he here?'

The man leads young Genevieve Krill away.

'Your heart was broken that day, Genevieve Krill,' says the spectral girl. 'You grew paranoid that Clogitt had set up the contest to steal a pack of magical mint humbugs from your house. There are no such things as magical mint humbugs. Trust me – I come from another realm. . .'

She glows brighter and is subsumed in a sphere of light, which fades to a pinprick and is gone.

'Krill!' roars a huge bearded man who has materialized from nowhere. He bounds towards you. 'Your cruelty to Bogg Clogitt has left him poor and hungry. Tut-tut, Krill, old girl! Come with me – to Christmas present!'

He grasps you, burying your face in his coat, and when he releases you, you emerge, gasping, outside a cottage. He beckons you to the window.

'Shut,' commands a man within, and at the sound of his voice a compartment in the wall clangs shut.

A woman places an envelope in a chest of drawers, which has a combination lock featuring symbols.

'I'll keep this safe and post it later, Bogg,' she trills. 'Lucky I always have questions on me, whose answers help me remember the combination.' She pats her pocket.

As they head out into the snow, oblivious to your presence, the bearded man mutters, 'You weren't meant to see that, Krill, old girl. Ah, well, his silly fault for not hiring the ghost of a few minutes after Christmas present.'

'You were *hired*?'

'I've said too much. Let's forget all that and. . .' – he throws open the cottage door – 'behold the poverty of the Clogitts!'

'Poverty, schmoverty! They were locking up valuables – they're probably worth millions!' You approach the compartment in the wall and say, 'Open'. It ignores you. 'Open up! Call yourself a door? More like a *prat*.' The door responds to Bogg Clogitt's voice only.

'Come on, old girl! When I told you to forget all that, I didn't mean forget about me saying, "Forget all that". Look at Bogg's <u>Christmas shopping list</u> – all it says is "Pot Noodles". It's all they can afford!'

'I bet it's those fancy king-size Pot Noodles.'

'Your cruelty to the Clogitts is sickening. It means that you'll be forgotten in the future while the Clogitts are revered! Imagine that! Give them all your money, Krill, and never think about humbugs again. Then you too will be admired by future generations!'

He vanishes into thin air. A silence descends. A hooded figure glides towards you. It seizes your arm painfully, and after a brief feeling of being trapped in a roaring whirlpool, you lurch to the ground. A curiously dressed person hails you.

'Welcome, stranger. I am Futuretron McGizmo. This cup holds all that remains of Julia Clogitt, history's greatest sculptor. Behind me is one of her masterworks, depicting Henry Kissinger.'

'What's this?' You fish out a note from among the bones.

''Twas found in her pocket.'

''Twas?'

'There's a big *'twas* revival in the future. Anyway, if you can answer Julia Clogitt's questions, I shall give you a pot of Future Ink which has the power to change words.'

1. Wayde van Niekerk broke the men's 400 metres record previously held by Michael Johnson; both of these men represented countries whose full names end in the same four letters. Which word (which is also the surname of the founders of a British company acquired by Coca-Cola in 2019) begins the name of the only other country to end in these letters?

2. Which word fills the blank space in these quotations, firstly from George Eliot's *Adam Bede* – 'When death, the great Reconciler, has come, it is never our tenderness that we _____ of, but our severity'. – and secondly from William Congreve's *The Old Bachelor* – 'Thus grief still treads upon the heels of pleasure: / Married in haste, we may _____ at leisure'?

3. Daniel Defoe (writing under the pseudonym 'The Scandalous Club') was an early practitioner of which profession? This profession is the title of a David Hare poem denouncing Boris Johnson as a 'straw-haired man' who 'gets high on repeating gratuitous advice', and consists of two five-letter words whose letters all occur within 'County Donegal'.

4. Which two-word phrase precedes 'Tour' to make the name of a reunion tour by the Sex Pistols? It appears in the King James Bible (such as in 'Likewise must the deacons be grave, not doubletongued, not given to much wine, not greedy of _____'), though in the New International Version it is usually rendered as 'dishonest gain'.

5. Which word precedes *of Mystery* to make the title of the first film released using a technology called Smell-O-Vision, in which odours were discharged into the cinema at appropriate moments, and *of a Woman* to make the title of the film which won Al Pacino his first Oscar?

Once you have answered these questions, Futuretron McGizmo solemnly hands you the ink. You pour some over the envelope reading 'Mind-bending master plan'. Before your eyes, the words transform. The handwriting remains the same, but 'Mind-bending' has become a hyphenated word meaning 'repairing a constraint', and 'master plan' has become a phrase meaning 'fellow made from a paste which hardens as it dries'.

A cat scurries across the floor. The sinister hooded figure, which has been beside you this whole time, chases it in rather undignified fashion, but flails in vain as the creature springs into the box at the base of the sculpture. With a flash of light, it has transformed into Henry's Cat, the title character of the 1980s children's cartoon. How astonishing! You remove your dress and toss it into the box, whereupon it turns into the American band Henry's Dress, who gaze around bemusedly. Surely this could only be the work of a sculptor aided by magical mint humbugs. . .

The hooded figure darts towards you, a gloved hand outstretched. 'Don't take me home yet!' you yell. 'I know you and your fellow ghosts were hired by the Clogitts to cheat me out of my money and distract me from the fact they stole my humbugs! I'm going to tell the ghost police!' Is there a ghost police? There must be, for the hooded figure recoils at the threat. 'Let me set things right,' you continue. 'I want to go back to the past, present and future one more time – then you can drop me off back in the present.' The hooded figure clicks his fingers and the other two ghosts appear; they confer in animated whispers. Then the young girl approaches.

You are back at the canine lookalike contest, at the same moment you had appeared last time. (The version of you and the ghostly girl who had previously appeared there are nowhere to be seen; it is odd how time travel works.)

**How do you ensure that your dog is the winner?** ㉔

The elderly man gives young Genevieve Krill the prize: an apple.

'This is Bogg Clogitt's apple,' he explains in response to her revolted gaze, as if this is a reassuring thing to hear. 'Everything about this apple is Bogg Clogitt's and will always pertain to Bogg Clogitt, whatever form it takes. It will be your privilege to possess it.'

'I'll be taking that, Genevieve!' you declare, leaping from behind the pillar and snatching the <u>apple</u>. 'I'm your future self – no time to explain! Actually, there's plenty of time to explain as I've got a trio of time-travelling ghosts, but I can't be bothered to. Bye! Hey, come here, Ghost of Christmas Present!'

The bearded man materializes, his expression suggesting that being at your beck and call is beneath his dignity.

He grasps you painfully tight and transports you back to the Clogitts' house in the present. You wait for them to leave and then open the door.

**Which four shapes form the combination to the Clogitts' chest of drawers?** ㉛

Inside the chest of drawers you find Julia's envelope, addressed to Eleanor Vibb, President of The Secret Sculpture Society. Within is a <u>photograph of Henry Kissinger</u> as well as the following note:

*Dear Eleanor,*

*Now you've got the block of stone I sent you, which I imbued with magic powers using the humbugs in our wall compartment that Bogg stole from that frightful Jennie Crawl or whatever her name is, you must work from this photo to make a sculpture and don't forget the box underneath! Then I'll take the credit for it, and I'll pay you with the cash that Bogg's planning to wheedle out of Crawl with some scheme about ghosts.*

*Julia*

**There is something you must do before you return to the future. In the future, you must ensure that you will be able to open the Clogitts' wall compartment when you go back to the present, so you can recover your humbugs. What course of action do you take?** ③②

# WINTERLUDE 2

*Answers on page 222*

'Must. . . get. . . humbugs!' you pant as you reach for them, but they, and the room around you, are retreating further and further away, as if whirling down an invisible plughole. Only darkness remains. Glittering fragments burst forth and form the face of Milbert.

'Good work, Miss Quincunx. But your next task may be a little thornier. Listen to this poem while you change into your new body. Each line is an anagram of a film which is set (at least partly) during the Christmas period – can you name the films?' He recites the poem in his frail, gentle voice, as if oblivious to how revolting it is.

> Relax, prophetess,
> Tart which I mess.
> Mess? Stress! Crave a thin
> Oily hand in
> The anal wig jelly.
> Stuff Rod in a wellie.
> The chrome act: a rump splits
> Beyond anal bits.

You ponder this foul poem as your surroundings swirl once more.

You begin to recite the answers, but your voice is deeper now, and this distracts you.

'I, er. . . awfully sorry for all this bumbling,' you say with a sheepish smile that feels rather out of character. Your hair has flopped over your eyes and you brush it away to see Milbert smiling at you adoringly. He gazes at you in dreamy silence for a few more seconds, then suddenly jolts out of his stupor.

'Right, then, Miss Quincunx... or should I call you Mister? I'll leave you to your next task, then. You do look quite charming. .'

His words fade, and his face disintegrates into a thousand dazzling lights.

# LOVE, FACTUALLY

*Hints on page 202*

*Answers on page 223*

A thousand cameras flash before your eyes. Your vision clears to reveal a room of journalists spread out before you.

'Prime Minister! Prime Minister!' they exclaim, each straining to raise their hand highest.

'Are you confident of getting a good deal with the US President?' one calls out.

'Would you say this is less of a special *treaty* for Britain,' interjects his neighbour, 'and more of a special *treat* for—'

'I was talking first, chicken-face!'

The two journalists wrestle each other to the ground; the second journalist overpowers the first.

'*You're* the chicken-face, chicken face!' shrieks the second journalist. 'I'm gonna make you squawk! Squawk for me, chicken!'

A short, slight young woman sitting beside you claps her hands. She wears a badge reading, 'Carla Masquill: Press Secretary'.

'Please, please, let's have no brawling! The Prime Minister's barely been in the job a week; the least you owe him is a little decorum.' With a tentative finger, her skin smooth as velvet, she strokes your arm and a heady thrill surges through you. 'Don't worry, Henry, you've got this,' she whispers.

A middle-aged man stands up and introduces himself.

'Barry Bitterbread of Bitterbread Management. My client, Juke Limburger, is soaring to the coveted Christmas number one spot with his megahit "Go Round the Big Hole". Mr Limburger used the Bitterbread rules of songwriting – and I demand, Prime Minister, that we use them to rewrite our behind-the-times, fuddy-duddy national anthem. You see, what you need for a hit is *nonsense*. But catchy nonsense. Why, with the help of my rules of songwriting, Mr Limburger compiled his lyrics entirely from words on his fridge magnets. See for yourself – with these seven simple rules, you can piece together Mr Limburger's song!'

## JUKE LIMBURGER'S FRIDGE MAGNETS

aunties      tiddlers

confessor

scissor      evidence      sickies

movable

echoing      backgammon

summoners

lettuces      turbogenerated

serrated      realism

czarism      splaying

## THE BITTERBREAD RULES

1. The last three words of the song all start with the same letter.

2. All evenly numbered words except one have the same number of letters.

3. The first six evenly numbered words are found in alphabetical order.

4. Two words which share the same third and fourth letter are found next to each other.

5. The longest word is six letters longer than the shorter of its two neighbours.

6. When two words end in the same three letters, the word which occurs earlier in alphabetical order must be placed first. These two words must not be placed within five words of each other (for example, if a word ending in 'ink' were in position 5, another word ending in 'ink' could not occupy position 1, 2, 3, 4, 6, 7, 8 or 9).

7. Each of the words in positions 5, 9 and 11 alphabetically precedes both of its neighbours; the words in positions 5, 9 and 11 also appear in alphabetical order.

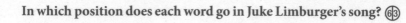

**In which position does each word go in Juke Limburger's song?** 63

| 1 | 2 | 3 | 4 | 5 | 6 | 7 | 8 |
|---|---|---|---|---|---|---|---|
| — | — | — | — | — | — | — | — |

| 9 | 10 | 11 | 12 | 13 | 14 | 15 | 16 |
|---|----|----|----|----|----|----|----|
| — | —  | —  | —  | —  | —  | —  | —  |

'The Prime Minister will respond to your proposal at the earliest convenience, Mr Bitterbread,' declares Carla. 'But we mustn't keep the President waiting.'

She ushers you out of the room into a vast, shiny airport terminal. The departures board reads:

**Destination**                                            **Flight Code**

| | | | | | | | | | | | | | | | | | | |
|---|---|---|---|---|---|---|---|---|---|---|---|---|---|---|---|---|---|---|
| A | N | G | L | E | S | E | Y |   |   |   |   |   |   |   |   | S | K | L |
| A | R | K | H | A | N | G | E | L | S | K |   |   |   |   |   | L | T | E |
| H | O |   | C | H | I |   | M | I | N | H |   | C | I | T | Y | V | O | G |
| B | A | R | K | I | N | G |   |   |   |   |   |   |   |   |   | L | E | G |
| D | A | R |   | E | S |   | S | A | L | A | A | M |   |   |   | D | R | E |
| D | O | W | N | H | A | M |   | M | A | R | K | E | T |   |   | G | N | A |
| N | E | W |   | C | A | L | E | D | O | N | I | A |   |   |   | W | E | R |
| K | R | A | S | N | O | Y | A | R | S | K |   |   |   |   |   | H | A | N |
| B | E | R | M | U | D | A |   |   |   |   |   |   |   |   |   | R | K | H |
|   |   |   |   |   |   |   |   |   |   |   |   |   |   |   |   | O | R | R |
|   |   |   |   |   |   |   |   |   |   |   |   |   |   |   |   | R | O | T |
|   |   |   |   |   |   |   |   |   |   |   |   |   |   |   |   | V | D | D |
|   |   |   |   |   |   |   |   |   |   |   |   |   |   |   |   | A | N | I |
| U | K |   | G | O | V | T |   | P | L | A | N | E |   |   |   | G | O | V |
|   |   |   |   |   |   |   |   |   |   |   |   |   |   |   |   | E | R | N |

A scruffy-haired young man accosts you.

'Prime Minister!' he gasps. 'You've been all over the world, right? Where should I go to see the most luscious babes? Shapely women drooling for a bit of English man-meat?' His hands undulate feverishly as he speaks, tracing the contours of an imaginary voluptuous woman over and over again.

'Kindly control yourself, sir,' says Carla. 'You're addressing the Prime Minister, a man of grandeur and poise, who never thinks about women in a sexual way even if they desperately want him to.'

'And why are some of the planes not shown on the departures board? What if the bustiest bombshells are waiting for me in one of those destinations and I'll never know! I wanna be like Juke Limburger, with super-hotties hanging on each arm and another one grafted onto my hip. It's driving me senseless!'

'The government plane,' Carla explains, 'carries the Prime Ministerial personage himself, and is of vital importance to the nation. It would be disrespectful to mention ordinary aircraft near it. If you wish, I will give you descriptions of the five missing destinations, in order.'

1. In 1990, a former nuclear physicist named André Gardes single-handedly attempted an armed invasion of this Channel Island. The island's name, being spelt identically to a Scots word for a garment, appears in the name of a ship which is named in honour of Robert Burns's poem *Tam o' Shanter*, in which a scantily clad witch dances in one such garment.

2. This French city is the setting for an Uwe Rosenberg-designed board game of the same name. The last four letters of the Roman counterpart to the goddess Athena followed by the first three letters of a character in Greek mythology described in Christopher Marlowe's *Doctor Faustus* as 'the face that launch'd a thousand ships' spell out this city's name backwards.

3. This Scottish town's name is formed from the initials of the actor (using the name by which she was credited in her films), who was the winner of the 2005 Screen Actors Guild Life Achievement Award, followed by the surname of the winner of the 2006 Screen Actors Guild Life Achievement Award; these actors played the title

roles in 1935's *Curly Top* and 1967's *Thoroughly Modern Millie* respectively.

4. This settlement in the Philippines, popular with tourists, is an anagram of the first name of Nikita Khrushchev's successor as First Secretary of the Communist Party of the Soviet Union. If the letter *d* in its name is replaced by *ñ*, it becomes the name of a climate pattern.

5. This island has a three-word name. In 1881, some women on this island gained the right to vote, making the Tynwald the first national parliament to grant women the vote in a general election. Ned Maddrell, who died in 1974, is believed to have been the last native speaker of this island's language, though the language has since been revived.

'I know where I'm going now!' the young sex maniac dribbles. 'I'm following Juke Limburger's advice!'

He bounds off, triumphant.

**Where is the man's destination?**                                    ㉜

A woman thunders to a man behind a desk, 'I need a ticket to the Land of Double Questions!'

'We don't have any flights there today,' protests the man.

'I demand it!' she continues. 'I demand it with every fibre of my being!'

A crowd has gathered round. She wheels round to address them.

'My butler has quit! He has returned to his native land, the Land of Double Questions. I must find him.'

'I shall be your butler!' shouts a butler in the crowd. 'I have a degree in Advanced Butlery from the University of—'

'Shut up, oaf!' roars the woman. 'I don't want any old butler – I plan to propose marriage to the man. Also, I wish him to resume his duties as my butler. Ever since I caught my husband entangled in the arms, legs and torso of another woman, I have lived a lonely life, brightened only by my brawny but incomprehensible manservant. When it was time for him to return home, I seized him in my arms and he asked a series of questions. I don't see their relevance, but I presume the poor wretch was wittering that he would miss me immensely and that, if I was amenable, he would fulfil me in a way which my previous husband never could and which will make my previous husband furiously jealous when I send him the recordings.'

'I have travelled to the Land of Double Questions!' proclaims a red-robed traveller with a long beard. 'It took me months to decipher their communication system. Whenever a citizen of that land asks you a pair of questions, you must answer neither question! The word indicated by each pair is made by eliminating the letters from the second answer which match those in the first answer. For instance, if a letter appears twice in the answer to the first question but three times in the answer to the second question, remove the first two instances of that letter from the answer to the second question. If the first question in the pair gives the answer "as" and the second question gives the answer "loaves", remove "as" from "loaves" to make the answer "love". Tell me, madam, what your butler asked.'

These are the questions she recounted:

1. Which word precedes both *Book* and *Lightning* in the titles of novels by Markus Zusak and Rick Riordan, and which word follows them?

2. Which word denotes a temple, a prominent example of which is depicted on the Cambodian flag, and which words fill the blank spaces in this extract from a *Lonely Planet* article describing how a COVID-19 outbreak in Cambodia was caused by 'a security breach that saw four visitors bribe their ____ ____ of a designated quarantine hotel'?

3. Which word meaning 'outer layer' is the stage name of the musician Deborah Dyer, and which word meaning 'removing the outer layer' can precede 'Bee' to make the name of either a Japanese band or an event where people gather to remove the chaff from maize?

4. Which word, found in the titles of a Red Hot Chili Peppers album containing 'Under the Bridge' and a David Morrell novel adapted into a 1982 Sylvester Stallone film, precedes

'flower' to make a name for *Asclepias curassavica*, and which seven-letter word means 'produced flowers', 'flourished' or, in the case of chocolate, 'developed a pale coating'?

5. Which words precede 'Something Good' in the title of a song written by Carole King and Gerry Goffin, and which word immediately precedes 'Life is your creation' in the lyrics to Aqua's 'Barbie Girl'?

6. In *Garner's Modern American Usage*, Bryan Garner defines two words as meaning, respectively, 'to disapprove earnestly' and 'to belittle, disparage' or 'to fall in value'. He argues that an expression meaning 'critical of oneself', which nowadays predominantly involves the first word, would be more correct if it involved the second (which used to be the more common form). What is the first word and what is the second?

7. In 2021, the Ealing comedy *Kind Hearts and Coronets* was named among the top ten British films by a magazine whose name contains which three-letter word (which, if it were absent, would make the magazine's name identical to that of an American magazine), and which part of the London borough of Ealing is also the surname of a Welsh goalkeeper who won the 1985 Football Writers' Association Footballer of the Year award?

8. Which word comes between 'spaghetti' and 'vongole' to complete the name of a popular Italian dish, as well as filling the blank in the title of the song 'Für _____, die' (also recorded in English as 'This Is for Everyone') by a band named after which Swiss-German artist,* whose works include *Twittering Machine* and *Ad Parnassum* and whose surname is German for 'clover'?

Having figured out the message, you hurry away to avoid the woman's reaction. But seconds later, you hear her bellow, 'Insolent

---

\* The artist's forename and surname will help you piece together your answer.

man! You dare suggest that my butler would insult me? He thinks of nothing but the nude pictures of me which I painted on his bedroom walls. Did my ex-husband send you because he couldn't bear the thought of me being buttled, a term which means "engaging in euphoric congress with a butler"? You're nothing but his spy – give me that false beard!'

'*OUCH!*'

Security officers scurry past you.

It's time for you to board the plane. Carla's eyes are moist as she bids you goodbye. Her hands tentatively reach up as if contemplating an embrace, but she thinks better of it, turns and walks away.

Negotiating the treaty is an exhausting, relentless task. When you return to 10 Downing Street, Carla is nowhere to be seen. You gaze out of the living room window. A man holding a stack of huge cards steels himself, then knocks on a door on the other side of the street.

A man opens the door. 'Hello, Uche!' he beams.

The man with the cards lurches back. 'Jules!' he gurgles. 'I thought Tracey was going to answer.'

'Why? There's no reason why Tracey would be more likely than me to open the door. No logical reason on earth. What's with the cards, pal?'

'They're not a confession of love!'

'I never thought they were.'

'Neither did I! Great minds, eh?'

'So what are the cards?'

'What cards? What are cards?'

'You don't know what *cards* are?'

'Oh, *cards*. I thought you said guards. These are a fun quiz game. Each card has one letter, two letters or three letters written on it. They're all numbered too, but don't worry about that – it's not like they spell a message when you read them in order! You ask me questions and I use the cards to piece answers together.'

Jules asks:

1. What nickname (which may be spelt with the third letter capitalized) is shared by an Australian physiotherapist who co-authored a book of 'Birth Skills' and a wide receiver who has broken various NFL records, including in 2018 becoming the youngest receiver with 1,500 receiving yards? It may also denote an object believed to possess magical powers or a genre of music associated with Shina Peters.

*Uche holds up card 10, then holds up card 10 again.*

2. Which two words, both ending in the same letter, fill the blanks in both of these quotations? Firstly, from Franklin D. Roosevelt: 'That is the spirit of Christmas, the \_\_\_\_\_ \_\_\_\_\_.' Secondly, from Ronald Reagan: 'But for many of us it's also a \_\_\_\_\_ \_\_\_\_\_, the birthday of the Prince of Peace'.

*Uche holds up card 19, then 14, then 7.*

3. What is the seven-letter title of an Eminem song, from the album *Music to Be Murdered By*, in which he describes his hatred of the violent title character? The NFL wide receiver mentioned in Question 1 added 'Schuster' to his surname in honour of a man who can be described by this word (in relation to the wide receiver).

*Uche holds up card 11, then 17, then 16, then 18.*

4. Which word for a duct leading from the kidney to the bladder or cloaca is an anagram of the surname of a news agency's German-born founder?

*Uche holds up card 9, then 13.*

5. A Haha Lung book subtitled *The Asian Art of the Ninja Masters* has what two-word title, which refers to 'the mental punch you never see coming'? A spoonerism of this title means 'discover a mass of water droplets in the air'.

*Uche holds up card 4, then 1, then 6, then 20.*

6. Which word precedes 'of Winchester' to complete the name of a conflict between the armies of Queen Matilda and Empress Matilda, which resulted in King Stephen being released from captivity? Some Americans pronounce a word meaning 'course' identically to this word.

*Uche holds up card 15, then 12.*

7. Which two Spanish words fill in the blanks in this quotation from the Argentinian writer Antonio Porchia: '*Todo está solo cuando _____ _____ solo*'? The quotation translates as 'Everything is alone when I am alone.'

*Uche holds up card 8, then 17, then 11, then 2.*

8. Which word fills both blank spaces in this extract from Robert Herrick's 'An Ode to Ben Jonson': 'Where we such clusters had / As made us nobly wild, not mad; / And yet each verse of thine / _____ the meat, _____ the frolic wine'? If this word is divided into two, each half fills a blank space in this quotation from a character in TV's *Agents of S.H.I.E.L.D.*: 'Whoever took this bullet _____ _____ an awful job'.

*Uche holds up card 3, then 20, then 5, then 1.*
'Hang on,' muses Jules. 'If you arrange these cards in numerical order. . .'
Uche yelps, hurls the cards away and careers off down the street.

**What message do the cards spell, when arranged in numerical order? The answer can be rendered, crossword-style, as (2, 3, 4, 2, 1, 3, 5, 4, 7, 4-4, 3), where the numbers in brackets represent word length and where punctuation is ignored.** ㊷

You enter your office. A beguiling scent reaches your Prime Ministerial nostrils. A card on your desk is imbued with Carla's delicate perfume.

You reach for it when—

'It's an international catastrophe!' yells a gaunt man, hurling open the door.

'What's happened?'

'Never in all my time as Downing Street chief of staff have I encountered such disaster,' says the man. 'I wanted to buy a Christmas gift for my girlfriend. But, looking furtively out of the shop window, who do I see but my wife, taking our six children on a shopping trip to get *me* a present! And behind them, also out shopping, are my husband and my fiancé, who from what I hear of their conversation turn out to be brothers, and they're each saying they want the other to meet me but don't realize they're talking about the same man. And then my widow – or at least she thinks she's my widow because I faked my death so she wouldn't twig that *I* was the mysterious lover her chiropractor was telling her about – is leading some kind of mourning parade with big banners showing pictures of my face, but before anyone can catch on, my boyfriend accidentally incinerates them with the flamethrower he promised to get me, which he's presumably taking to the repair shop run by my friend with benefits. So I've got to get the present pronto and sneak away unnoticed or all hell will break loose! But the dithering man in the accessories shop won't even tell me the names of what he's selling; he just *describes* each one at length. And my girlfriend, the sensual little rascal, has told me she wants something *unique* or our relationship is over! If any sentence that the man in the accessories shop uses to describe a potential present can also apply to another present in the shop, I'm not allowed to get her either present. So I just bought all of them, proposed to the man in the shop and skedaddled! Tell me, Prime Minister, which present should I give my girlfriend? Here are the man's descriptions. . .'

1. The absorbency of these items is measured by the Rothwell scale. They are an anagram of 'canned inspection'.

2. This item has eleven letters. According to British *GQ* magazine, it 'will elevate your outfit. Just ask Tyler, The Creator', while *The Rake* magazine describes it as 'the cravat's casual, rustic cousin'.

3. This is a three-letter item of sporting equipment. It may precede 'boots', 'pole' or 'jumper'.

4. This item is mentioned in the *Odyssey*, in which Odysseus is instructed to take one such item to people who, knowing nothing of the sea, mistake it for a winnowing fan. In *The Talented Mr. Ripley*, Ripley murders Dickie Greenleaf with one. In Lord Byron's *Childe Harold's Pilgrimage*, it follows 'There breathes a living fragrance from the shore, / Of flowers yet fresh with childhood; on the ear / Drops the light drip of the suspended [. . .]'.

5. What I'm describing begins with the name of an important political figure in French history who lived from the eighteenth to the early nineteenth century. They are coins once used in France, though the name may also refer to pastries similar to *mille-feuilles*.

6. What I'm describing contains the name of a metallic chemical element. Consisting of two words of equal length, it refers to fine particles, and something is compared to this item if it is in demand and difficult to obtain.

7. These items contain the papal name of a Roman Catholic pope who died during the twentieth century (though the name has also been used by earlier popes). The items – if their final *s* is removed – precede 'mate' to make a checkmate pattern involving the king being trapped by his own pieces (most commonly a rook on either side) giving the impression that he is wearing these items, which have a French-derived name.

8. This item contains the title of a Best Picture Oscar-nominated film from the 2000s. Richard Dreyfuss claimed that Bill Murray got drunk and threw one such item at him, and the item becomes a word meaning 'off the right path' if one letter is removed.

**Which item would the chief of staff's girlfriend most appreciate from him?**

The chief of staff leaves. You snatch up Carla's card. It reads:

*Dear Henry,*

*In tomorrow's press conference they will ask about every detail of the treaty. I've written you a little quiz to help you remember.*

1. To prevent linguistic misunderstandings between British and American speakers, which word should from this day forth be used as a greeting, such that if a person forgetfully uses the word 'hello' instead, all others must stare at them as if they've talked liké Chaucer for no reason at all? It is the surname of a man who shared the 1996 Nobel Prize in chemistry, follows 'Rip' to complete the name of a company which makes clothes and accessories for surfers, and has meanings including 'ringlet'.

2. If one country is deemed to have wronged the other, the current president or monarch of the country in the wrong must in penance change their name to what? This first name is shared by the man who led the victorious forces at the Battle of Cannae, an American comedian who helped bring to public attention the rape accusations against Bill Cosby and a villain who first appeared in the novel *Red Dragon*.

3. Disputes between the two countries will be settled by a jury of women who share which first name, which is found within the name of an African country? If the first letter of the name is moved back one place in the alphabet (that is, so that *b* becomes *a*, for example) and spaces are inserted, it becomes the abbreviated name of a London museum.

4. The friendship between the two countries will be celebrated annually with a fayre held on a specially constructed platform in the Atlantic Ocean halfway between London and Washington, D.C. The main event will be a competition to find the best lookalike of which character, whose real name is never revealed either in the novel in

which he first appears or in its 1964 film adaptation? In the novel (but not in the film), he is a karate expert with a cleft palate and a fondness for eating cats; in the film (but not in the novel), he dies by electrocution.

5. In all official meetings between the two countries' heads of government, all those present must be dressed as which character? A syndrome in which a person who has consumed hair develops a gastric hairball is named after this character; a Disney film was also intended to be named after her, but the name was changed apparently because having a girl as the title character was deemed unappealing to boys.

6. All such official meetings must include the heads of government holding hands, looking each other in the eye and repeating which word, gradually increasing in volume? This word, which is the title of a Bob Dylan album, fills the fourth blank space in this quotation from a play – 'They told me to take ＿＿＿ ＿＿＿ ＿＿＿ ＿＿＿, and then transfer to one called Cemeteries and ride six blocks and get off at – Elysian Fields!' – where the four missing words are also the play's title.

The note continues:

*Finally, I must tell you that I am leaving your services. It pains me to confess, but my feelings for you have become more than professional, and I cannot hope to imagine that they are reciprocated. Tonight, before I depart to become a hermit, I shall attend my niece's Christmas play. I am so embarrassed by this admission of love that I cannot show my face. I shall wear an animal costume and, being small and dainty, shall be mistaken for a child. If (I hope against hope!) you do have feelings for me, come and find me before it is too late.*

 *Take all the first, then all the last*
 *From the last two rounds.*
 *I am the odd one out.*
 *Forever yours,*
   *Carla*

You summon your driver and demand to be escorted to the theatre. You are seized with an overwhelming desire to propose to Carla.

**But which one is Carla? If you make the wrong choice, you will have proposed marriage to a stranger's child and your political career will be over.** 53

# WINTERLUDE 3

*Answers on page 227*

'Transport me to everlasting raptures and marry me!' you exclaim as the costumed figure begins to remove its mask – but it vanishes as Milbert appears in the blackness before you. 'Come, Miss Quincunx. Absorb yourself in these questions as you prepare for your next quest.' Each is the title of a UK Christmas number one song, with each word – except for 'the', 'in', 'to' and 'of' – replaced by a synonym (which may be inappropriate to the context). Identify the eight songs.

1. Howdy, farewell
2. Ecological, ecological turf of dwelling
3. Myself determination invariably zero thee
4. Yield to transmitter
5. Satellite waterway
6. Sturdy of the clandestine
7. Additional block in the obstruction (separate couple)
8. Soil strain

By the time you are finished, you are in your old body once again. You feel rugged ground beneath you. Milbert still stands beside you, looking rather nonplussed.

'It seems, Miss Quincunx, that I'm going to stay visible for longer than I'd planned. A pity, rather – I'd been hoping to pick my nose unnoticed. But you've seen enough revolting things in your dimension not to mind.' He inserts a bony finger up his nostril and waggles it at great length and with great concentration. 'I'll not offer my help until you need it,' he declares once he has finally finished.

# THE CHRISTMAS BEFORE

*Hint on page 203*

*Answers on page 228*

You and Milbert are standing on a narrow trail snaking up a craggy mountain. Night is coming.

'Is anybody there?' calls a weak, desperate voice. 'Help me! I've been here for ages. . . my name's Jim. . .'

'Jim? Jim!' yells Milbert. 'That wonderful man must have escaped the locked dimension somehow! Thank merciful heavens and let jingle bells ring! I'm coming for you, Jim, old buddy!'

He scrambles up the path, losing his footing several times. Stones crumble beneath his scurrying feet and fall into the silent void. You follow slowly, gripping the mountainside.

The path twists to reveal a man chained to a rock.

'He's just a different man named Jim,' Milbert mutters. 'I should have known. Still, we must help him.'

This other Jim's eyes bulge. '*Oh no! They're coming!*'

You follow his gaze. You can make nothing out in the blue-black sky. As he winces and squirms, you finally discern a pair of brightly coloured specks growing larger. Lovebirds. His shrieks fill the air as the creatures alight upon him, hop along his belly and, with sudden frenzy, tear into his chest. They depart into the night, the man's heart dangling from their claws.

'Perhaps we can free him from his chains,' sighs Milbert. 'Give him a decent burial.'

The chains hold fast.

'They will not break,' croaks a voice. You and Milbert leap up with a start. The man is alive.

'It grows back every time,' he continues. You peer into the gory cavern in his chest and spy a heart the size of a rosehip. 'It'll be fully grown by next Christmas – nice and plump for the birds to take. They came for my heart the Christmas before – then they gave it to someone who gave it away. When this heart is given to someone special, I'll finally be free. If I cry out the name of my special somebody when the lovebirds arrive, they must convey the heart to that person. I'm sure it was my special somebody who sent me this Christmas card.'

Pressed between a chain and the rock is a yellowing, tattered card. The outside shows visual clues (mostly soundalike clues) to the titles of films. 'They may not all be romance films *per se*,' says Jim, 'but they all have romantic themes. And look at these sentences inside the card. In each one, a string of letters has been missed out, which may contain spaces and punctuation. Each of these strings of letters (once spaces and punctuation are removed) spells out a term of endearment! Whoever has enticed me with such wordplay is my special one, I have no doubt.'

1. (1958)

2. (2007)

3. (1995)

perdue
verloren
perdidos

4. (2003)

5. (1993)

6. (1945)

7. (2009)

Inside the card is written:

1. Though my dogs may greet you with a fierce snarer pendants have a curious habit of calming them: simply dangle one such object in front of them and they will be mesmerized by the sight of the fossilized resin.

2. As soon as I heard the bell marking the start of the periodic table quiz clement-related facts entirely vanished from my mind.

3. Please stop asking me if I have any knitting needles, for you know full well that the only things I own which are long and less than half an inch wiring and spaghetti.

4. Although my father dreams that I will someday make my fortune – and his fame – accompanying his poetry recitals by playing the tugging seems to me a less demeaning way of earning money.

5. A woman wearing an ill-fitting caked me into joining her 'Superhero Club'.

6. My mother intended me to see the censored version of *The Texas Chainsaw Massacre*, in which no murder is ever committed nor so much as hinted at, but since she inadvertently took me to see the version that was unmerged from the cinema resolved to become a serial killer.

7. I still don't understand why you sour dazzling torch into my eyes when all I wanted was to have a moment of quiet in the gloom.

'I've narrowed it down to six people,' says Jim. 'Each one either only lies or only tells the truth. No-one refers to themselves in the third person. No-one has more than one name, no two people share a name, nor does anyone mention a person who is not among these six. You will never find out the names of two people, but that will not hinder your attempts to find my special somebody. No-one is capable of making a paradoxical statement such as "this sentence is false". Long ago, I asked each of them if they wrote the card. I'll tell you their names and what they said – then you'll be able to help me work it out. Firstly. . .' He stops and shudders at the distant, shrill chirp of a lovebird. 'No. . . the lovebirds will not let me divulge the six people's names and their statements. Instead, I'll ask you questions. You can piece together the six people's statements from their answers; each set of answers can be divided into either two or three sentences.'

### PERSON A:

1. Which name, which may be spelt backwards to produce the surname of a science fiction author, is that of a huge turtle which is the title character of an Ernest Borgnine film? It is also a word meaning a pure form of honey used in pharmaceuticals, and is spelt identically to the word for honey in Latin, Catalan and Portuguese.

2. Which word concludes the names of an oxymoronically titled TV series starring Reese Witherspoon and Nicole Kidman and an oxymoronically titled Arnold Schwarzenegger film with the tagline 'When he said I Do, he never said what he did'?

3. What are the last two words of both a single by T.I. featuring Eminem from the album *No Mercy* and a TV detective series whose central character is the author of works including *The Corpse Danced at Midnight*?

4. If the first word of a catchphrase used by a pair of brothers is replaced by its opposite, it becomes the name of a Beatles song containing the lyrics 'I've got lips that long to kiss you'. Which two words do they both end in?

5. Which words follow 'Jesus said unto them, Verily, verily, I say unto you, Before Abraham was,' to complete a quotation from the Gospel of John (King James Version) which has been interpreted as a claim to divinity? They precede a word meaning 'traditional and unauthenticated story' and an alter ego of Beyoncé to make the titles of a Richard Matheson novel and a Beyoncé album respectively.

6. The name of which chain of French bakeries is also the first name of the title character of an 1830 novel, which begins 'It was a dark and stormy night', and the surname of the driver of the car in which Princess Diana was fatally injured?

## PERSON B:

1. Which title is shared by a film in which George Formby plays a man falsely accused of murder and a Disney TV series about competitive twins? It is also a catchphrase which catapults Bart Simpson to fame when he appears on *The Krusty the Clown Show*.

2. Which two words follow 'He's' to make the title of a Bee Gees song, 'Fear is' to make the title of a Zach Williams song, 'I'm Not Calling You' to make the title of a Florence and the Machine song and 'If a man say, I love God, and hateth his brother, he is' to make a quotation from the King James Bible?

3. Which palindrome does the letter 'D' stand for in the racing abbreviation DNF?

4. The Psammead, which grants wishes, and an evil being which appears in Derry, Maine, and whose aliases include Bob Gray are both identified by what name in book titles?

## PERSON C:

1. With which four words does the title character of a Shel Silverstein song introduce himself to his father before continuing, 'How do you do! Now you're gonna die!'?

2. *Jacques a dit* is the French equivalent of which game, traditionally played by children?

3. Which four words used in a courtroom oath are an anagram of 'thought ninth butter'?

1. Which chat show, which ran for a single series in 2015, was named after its two presenters and featured cookery alongside the chat, a similar format to the presenters' late-nineties collaboration *Light Lunch*? These two presenters announced that they were quitting a different show by releasing a joint statement including the words 'We're not going with the dough'.

2. Which two words follow 'Why Americans' to complete the headline of a *Washington Post* article which concludes by warning of the consequences 'if we keep expecting students who can't construct decent sentences to magically produce coherent essays'? They also fill the blank space in this quotation from Frank Zappa: 'Most rock journalism is people who ____, interviewing people who can't talk, for people who can't read.'

3. Which three words, which appear in the title of a Bertrand Russell essay in which he explains the reasons for his atheism and his belief that Jesus was not 'the best and wisest of men', precede *Spock* to make the title of Leonard Nimoy's first autobiography and *Your Negro* to make the title of a documentary inspired by James Baldwin's unfinished book *Remember This House?*

4. Two singer-songwriters, one of whom penned a song in which he gives advice to Jack, Stan, Roy, Gus and Lee and the other penned a song which prompted Warren Beatty to say, 'Let's be honest. That song was about me', share which surname?

1. Which two words precede 'Live' to make a live album by a former member of the Beatles, whose title and cover artwork reference a conspiracy theory that he died and was replaced by a lookalike?

2. Which two words follow 'The Death of' to make the title of an essay on literary criticism by Roland Barthes? The essay's title (as it appeared in the original French) was a pun on Sir Thomas Malory's retellings of Arthurian legends.

3. Which three-letter first name is shared by a man nick-named 'The Velvet Fog', who co-wrote 'The Christmas Song', and a voice actor whose roles included Barney Rubble and Bugs Bunny?

4. Which two words conclude the title of a single by Pulp which was named after a working title of a James Bond film (the first Eon Productions Bond film whose title does not refer to Ian Fleming's life or work), though it was rejected as the film's theme tune? The film's final title uses the letter D instead of the letter L, but is otherwise spelt identically to the aforementioned working title.

5. What is the short first name of a basketball player who in 2018 won her fourth World Cup gold medal and in 2021 won her fifth Olympic gold medal? She and Megan Rapinoe were the first same-sex couple to appear on the cover of *ESPN The Magazine*'s *Body Issue*. This name is also a legal term ultimately derived from a Latin verb meaning 'follow'.

6. Which two words should fill the blank space in this quota-tion from Oscar Wilde's 'The True Function and Value of Criticism': 'Anybody can make history. Only a great man _____ it'?

### PERSON F:

1. Which two words precede 'the damn bill!' to make a response uttered by Bernie Sanders during a heated debate about healthcare, which became a meme, and follow *The Play What* to make a theatrical tribute to Morecambe and Wise?

2. The title of which Arnold Bennett novel, which is subtitled 'A Story of Adventure in the Five Towns', may precede

*Players* to make a series of Cézanne paintings, one of which was sold for a record-breaking price to the royal family of Qatar?

3. Which two words conclude the title of the Arctic Monkeys' debut album and begin the title of a film in which Christian Bale, Cate Blanchett and Heath Ledger are among actors playing characters inspired by the same man?

4. Which name follows 'Mary' to make a derogatory term for a flawless character in fan fiction and 'Peggy' to make the name of a song recorded by Buddy Holly?

5. Which short first name is shared by the directors of the films *Bean*, *Hacksaw Ridge* and *High Anxiety*?

6. The three kinds of which plural noun include a branch of mathematics dealing with numerical data, according to a quotation which Mark Twain, probably erroneously, described as a 'remark attributed to Disraeli'?

**Who is Jim's special somebody, and which letter does his special somebody correspond to?** ⑤③

# WINTERLUDE 4

*Answers on page 231*

The sky becomes a neon haze of lovebird colours, green, yellow and orange, and distorted, piercing chirps echo through the air. 'You are about to enter an unusual dimension indeed, Miss Quincunx,' says Milbert. 'Who knows, it may even be to your taste. Even if it's not, we must get our Jim back! Listen now – this will prepare you for what's in store. . .'

> Here's a puzzle as knotty as tangled bootlaces:
> The twenty-four words that should fill these blank spaces
> Can be grouped into eight sets of three anagrams
> Such as 'swine', 'wines' and 'sinew', or 'arms', 'mars' and 'rams'.

> Let's _____, then, Mr Grod:
> You really are so foul,
> You're as dire as tennis _____
> Or an _____ in the _____,
> Mr Grod!

> You're a mean one, Mr Grod!
> While you _____ on tenderloins
> You _____ your guests some _____ crumbs
> On _____ the size of coins,
> Mr Grod!

> You're a _____ one, Mr Grod!
> _____ _____* to this _____.
> Your manners are _____ the belt,
> Your scheming's even worse,
> Mr Grod!

* * * * * * * * * * * * * * * * * * * * * * * * * * * * * * * * * * * * * *

\* The order of these two words may be reversed. It's entirely irrelevant which one comes first.

47

You're a rotter, Mr Grod!
You joyless Christmas-_____,
You're not a wholly human _____,
You're _____alligator,
Mr Grod!

You're a stinker, Mr Grod!
You _____your ele-floots
To _____ _____ from the trees.
What nauseating brutes!
Mr Grod!

You're a killjoy, Mr Grod!
If Venns are gathering roses
You tear off all the _____
Which you _____ to their noses,
Mr Grod!

You're a vile one, Mr Grod!
All you love is filthy _____,
Your _____'s the coldest thing on _____,
Your soul's like a verruca,
Mr Grod!

Have half a point for each correct answer in this round.

When you have completed the puzzle, you look down to discover that your torso is striped and aubergine-shaped and your limbs are thin and rubbery, with a fine coating of bright fur.

'What in the name of confounded contortion?
My body's distorted beyond all proportion!
But hang on a minute, I'm talking in rhyme!
What creature am I, to screech rhymes the whole time?'

'You are a Venn, Miss Quincunx. One of a great many little creatures preparing to celebrate the festive season.'

# THE GROD WHO OBLITERATED CHRISTMAS

*Hints on page 203*

*Answers on page 232*

*All the Venns down in Vennburg liked Christmas a lot,*
*But the Grod, who lived south-west of Vennburg, did not!*
*The Grod was the host of the Vennburg pub quiz.*
*There was never a quiz quite as fiendish as his,*
*It made Venns scratch their heads like their heads had got lice*
*(And some used a high-speed head-scratching device).*
*But each Christmas the Venns sat and carved the roast beast.*
*They did not want a quiz, they did not in the least!*
*They passed the time gobbling and furiously bickering*
*With an elderly aunt with a parrot called Chickering.*
*And the Grod fumed with rage from his head to his boots*
*In a cave which he shared with some wild ele-floots.*
*(For, to him, sneaky riddles and cryptograms seemed*
*Like oxygen, lifeblood, like treasures undreamed.)*
*Then he had an idea! With a smirk most unpleasant,*
*He muttered, 'I'll show them! I'll steal all their presents!*
*Then I'll set those Venns clues to the presents' location*
*And traps to catch Venns when they lack concentration.*
*And instead of their dreadful rejoicing and guzzling*
*They will spend Christmas Day quizzing, riddling and puzzling!'*

ELE-FLOOTS

Unutterably vile was the Grod's great brainwave.
Riding a ramshackle sleigh from his cave
To the town, with a titter he slid down each chimmer-ney.
Sneaky Grod! He's as lethal as lead or antimony!
He snatched all their gifts! And the Venns the next morn
Found that their houses were bare and forlorn.
On Mount Scowling, the Grod through his megaphone boomed:
'Hello, Venns! Find your presents or Christmas is doomed!
Every Venn with a taste for inane holidays,
Find your way to the centre of Vennburg Hedge Maze!'
For that's where he'd carved every word on this page
Under the spell of delight tinged with rage.
'Place each line's first letter, in order, between
Letters of answers to questions most mean!
Next, add in some spaces and you've got a clue
Guiding you on to the gifts you are due!
Roll on, Round 1 – it's been waiting for you. . .'

1. This nickname a catcher in baseball did share
   With the name of a fictional food-snatching bear.

2. This word means 'perform', though sometimes it means 'dosh
   That is paid for a journey', or 'diet or nosh'.

3. This word's found in the name of a show with John Reese;
   It's that feeling when boredom and apathy cease.

4. This hero of Goethe's is very downbeat;
   His name's shared with a town where they once made a sweet.

5. This begins two book titles, by Steinbeck and Maugham,
   About Lennie and Philip, who do not conform.

6. A maths whiz by this surname once lived in Bordeaux.
   It means 'layout' if one letter's swapped for an 'o'.

7. This means 'plant' if said one way; if you say it another,
   You're left with a word which refers to Babe's mother.

   **Find the place on the map where your gifts are located –**
   **Your holiday frolics may not be frustrated!**

'Now you know where to go! But stop! Hold your horses!
While you racked your slack brains, I sent advance forces
Of ele-floots pinning down devious drawings,
And half of those drawings hide, under their moorings,
Eight landmines to blow you to extra-fine powder
(Which I'll keep in a tin and I'll sprinkle on chowder).
The drawings I've booby-trapped perfectly match
The answers to eight fiendish questions I've hatched,
In which I'll give you clues to three things in a sequence
And the thing that comes next is the answer! So seek, once
You've found the eight death traps, the fastest safe path.
But be careful – there may be a grim aftermath.
The clues drawn on safe sheets you cross on your passage,
Will sound out, in order, a judicious message.'

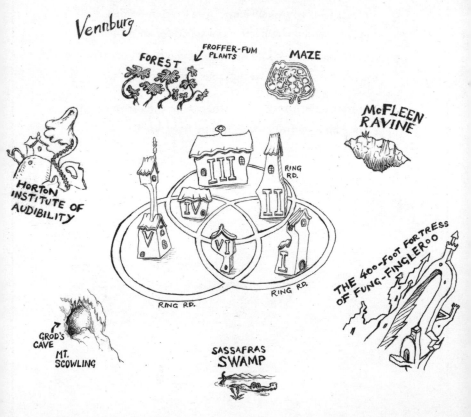

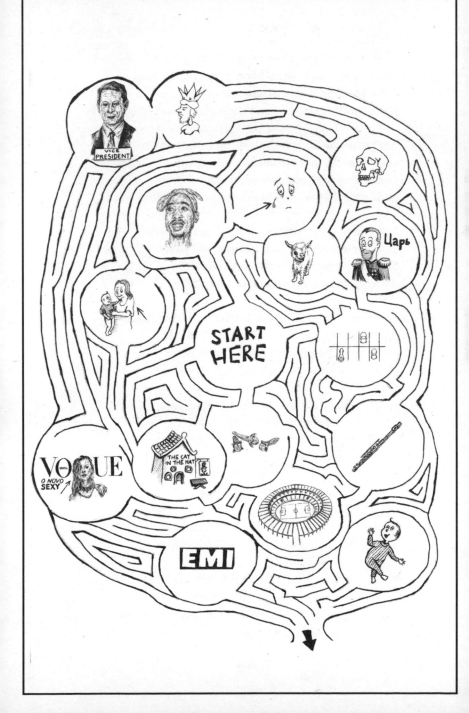

## ROUND 2:

1. First's a parent (or surname – it's businessman Jack's),
   Then what comes after Maasai or Rooney or Max,
   Third's a singular instrument meant to be shaken.
   If you work out the fourth, you might just save your bacon!

2. Your first clue is Loki – how fittingly tricksy!
   (I think of myself as a mischievous pixie.)
   Game is up next, and then Aggi is third.
   Now what do you think? Can you find the fourth word?

3. Listen closely, so you can traverse my minefield:
   First comes a spear which Romans did yield.
   Second's a note that's between so and ti.
   Third comes a system that followed XP.

4. Let's begin with a man who is known as Slim Shady,
   And follow him up with a Turkish First Lady.
   Third comes an artist who grew up in Kent,
   Who wrote all her bedfellows' names in a tent.

5. In this sequence, a female canine comes first,
   Second is someone in ardour submersed,
   Third is a person who's still in their youth.
   You must find what comes fourth, like a sharp-witted sleuth!

6. First's a Jewish co-founder of modern Iraq,
   Then a hairstylist: angled bobs formed his trademark
   And Satan's spawn's mum used his style in a chiller.
   Third is the author of *The City and the Pillar*.

7. This spot (though not literally) swings, is like fire.
   Next comes a small shop selling stylish attire.
   Third's a place you can stay, which is found at resorts,
   Whose colour is that of cured ham or rose quartz.

**8.** An instrument's first – it's a pair of short sticks,
Then a duchy that's linked to the fourth one of six
(Whose husband, it's said, had a temper quite fiery).
Third come Cussler, Sinclair, Barker, Owen and Myrie.

**Are you out of the maze? Is your brain overloaded?
Tell me the message that you have decoded.**

*When the Venns reached the presents, how great was their gladness!*
*They sang carols and chants, they sang 'Our House' by Madness.*
*But their jollity turned to confusion and dread.*
*The name-tags were gone! There were clues there instead!*
*Then the Grod took his megaphone. 'Yoo-hoo! There's news!*
*You will know whose is whose from my devious clues*
*To names which are found in these pages of rhyme,*
*Some forwards, some backwards. So, "lemony lime"*
*Has "Emily" squirrelled inside, in reverse.*
*There are two names that cannot be found in my verse:*
*These are the names of the two Venns whose presents*
*Have been sneakily swapped out for something less pleasant.*
*You only need scour through the parts in italics,'*
*Said that dastardly Grod, idly coiling his hallux,*
*'But also check pages that we've yet to reach!'*
*And thus, as the Venns gawped, he finished his speech.*

## ROUND 3:

1. This name's shared by a girl with whom Lear got quite huffy
   And the cheerleading sidekick of Angel and Buffy.

2. There are three sportsmen who found great acclaim
   And, though you may call each of them by this name,
   Use their nicknames to make your address sound more breezy:
   Mr. Cub, Swervin' Irvan, and the Big Easy.

3. A *Lion King* character goes by this name
   Which is spelt, not pronounced, exactly the same
   As a man who is named in a Shakespeare play's title,
   Who, betrayed by false friends, escapes all things societal.

4. This name's shared by someone who played George the Third's wife
   And the socialist author of *The Story of My Life*.

5. A Bible book which doesn't mention God's name
   Shares this name with a certain Childline-founding dame.

6. This name – of a host of *This Morning* and model,
   Whose shenanigans Barlow believed to be twaddle –
   Starts the stage surname of someone whose work
   Includes *Days and Nights*, *Bridge of Spies* and *Dunkirk*.

7. This name's shared by an actress who wrote *Wishful Drinking*
   And a girl in a book who can move things by thinking.

8. A princess to whom Lone Starr has shown his medallion
   Shares this name with a scooter that's 'wasp' in Italian.

9. You will get, if both halves of this girl's name change places,
   Part of Yorkshire, or being a jockey in races.

10. A musician thus named wrote 'No More Sad Refrains'.
    Her name means 'light brown' or 'resembling grains'.

11. You've a Greek god's name here; if his last letter flits
    To the front, it's a place no direct sunlight hits.

12. This is the name of a lumberjack fond
    Of cross-dressing, as well as Nick Saloman's frond.

13. A Dumas book title thus names a French queen.
    Her namesake played Flopsy and Doctor Harleen.

14. This name's borne by a Bond girl who walked from the sea.
    Make a phrase if you add the word 'bun', 'trap' or 'bee'.

15. This name can mean God granting sinners a blessing;
    Someone by this name's played by Debra Messing.

16. This name's shared by a man whom Ivanka Trump wed
    And one who, at nine hundred and sixty-two, dropped down dead.

**Which Venns, if they heeded their lust to unwrap
Irresistible gifts, would be caught in my trap?**

*The Venns solved the clues! They were quick as two flashes,*
*But the presents they opened contained only ashes!*
*'I've burnt all your gifts!' shrieked the Grod, thrilled and rapt.*
*And in each Venn in Vennburg that day. . . something snapped.*
*They gathered their weapons, their rackets and knives,*
*And an aged Venn-gardener sharpened her chives.*
*Those frothing Grod-mobbers ascended Mount Scowling,*
*Brains brimming with dreams of most dire disembowelling,*
*When the Grod pulled a lever and plunged them into*
*A pit full of short-tailed rock crabs and a gnu.*
*'We're trapped!' wailed a Venn with a toy slug named Numan.*
*Then that ghastly Grod spoke, with a grin most inhuman:*
*'Your festering maw oozes putrid claptrap!*
*You've the world to explore! See, I've left you a map!*
*But beware: it's a map that explodes when it's pressed*
*And it seems you've not brought an explosion-proof vest.*
*On this map of the world, there's one safe place to push*
*That opens a tunnel that leads to a bush.*
*Your finger, if freedom's your wish, should come down*
*On an isle that belongs in the centre of town. . .'*

### ROUND 4:

I.  Eric Heiden excelled where this word precedes 'skating';
    You will have many chats if this word precedes 'dating'.

II. A young Venn who wails while I play my Grod game
    Possesses a plaything that's known by this name.

III. Take 'Me' from a battle where Rome vanquished Carthage
    For this sign of a cause of some china-shop carnage.

IV. With nieces and nephews a woman swaps curses.
    Her bird has this name, found in previous verses.

V.  In severe epilepsy, this word precedes 'mal'.
    It is found in the name of the longest canal.

VI. This might follow 'football' or 'record' or 'fiddle';
    In Ernest Cline's title, it's found in the middle.

**So those are the questions – you've had time to read 'em.**
**What is the island that leads you to freedom?**

## EPILOGUE:

*The Venns found the tunnel and made their escape*
*And they staggered back home through the joyless landscape.*
*They sat on their beanbags bereft of festivity*
*And tried to think up some distracting activity.*
*Then a small Venn piped up, 'Even though all that quizzing*
*Was riling and peeving, it's left my brain fizzing!*
*It is hard to admit, but I'm craving more puzzles*
*Like a gluttonous wolf craves the sheep that it guzzles.'*
*So they called to the Grod, 'Do you have quizzes spare?'*
*And the Grod very languidly strolled from his lair.*
*Yes, he did have spare quizzes! In fact he had eight.*
*And the Venns strained to solve them until it grew late*
*When, contentedly, off they meandered to bed.*
*Thenceforth, Christmas was off. They held quizzes instead.*

# WINTERLUDE 5

*Answers on page 235*

'Last time round, you said that horrible dimension might be *to my taste*,' you expostulate. 'If I ever say a rhyme again, even by accident, I will physically vomit! And I'd gladly vomit all over you, you uncaring—'

'With each new adventure, we're one step closer to saving Jim!'

'Jim, Jim, Jim – knickers to Jim! All you do is pack me off from one dimension to the next, full of flesh-eating birds and traps and endless rhymes, and as soon as I stagger out, you're all, "Oh, good, soon I'll see lovely Jim!" Not "How are you, Miss Quincunx?" or "You look a bit battered about, Miss Quincunx, how about a nice cup of whatever it is they serve in the void between dimensions?" What do you plan to do with me after we do the dozen anyway?'

'Oh, we probably won't – odds are, you'll be killed,' he replies, as if he expects you to be reassured by this. 'Take your next quest, for instance – there's a villain who'll stop at nothing to carry out his dastardly plan. Let's get into the mood with a bit of panto, shall we?'

1. Which Shane Meadows film spawned three TV miniseries, set in 1986, 1988 and 1990 respectively?

'Oh, no, it isn't!' exclaims Milbert when you tell him the answer. The man is *exasperating*.

2. Which proverb, expressing hope that things will get better in the future, forms the last four words in both the novel and the film *Gone with the Wind*?

'Oh, no, it isn't!' exclaims Milbert once again when you tell him the answer.

3. *Now?*, *The Fantastic Journey* and *In Hollywood* conclude the titles of the second, third and fourth instalments of which book series?

When you tell Milbert the answer, he cries out, 'He's behind you!' If you suddenly exploded, you think to yourself, he'd barely bat an eyelid as long as it didn't get in the way of reuniting him with his beloved Jim.

4. 'You told me that you didn't love him / And you were gonna say goodbye / But if you really didn't mean it / Why did you have to lie?' and 'Can you practice what you preachin'? / Would you turn the other cheek again?' are lyrics from songs recorded respectively by Roberta Flack and Donny Hathaway, and the Black Eyed Peas, which share what title?

'It's behind you!' shrieks Milbert when you announce the answer.

5. Which six words, which have since become a proverb, fill in the blank space in this quotation from Polonius in *Hamlet*? 'Therefore, since _____, / And tediousness the limbs and outward flourishes, / I will be brief: your noble son is mad'?

'Oh, no, it isn't!' bellows Milbert as soon as he hears the answer. He's really getting into the spirit of things. This is worse than rhyming.

6. Which Netflix series, which ran from 2013 to 2019, was described by *Rolling Stone* as 'not just a popular show but a historic event: It has *ladies* in it. Ladies who are doing things we never see ladies in entertainment do'?

'Oh, no, it isn't!' repeats Milbert when you say the answer.

7. George Clooney, having been told that the character he was to play was 'a hick', asked his uncle in Kentucky to read the script for which film into a tape recorder, from

which Clooney learnt his lines? It was only when the Coen Brothers demanded to know why he'd changed the script that he discovered that his uncle had omitted every mention of the words 'damn' and 'hell'.

When you answer, Milbert cries out, 'He's behind you!'

8. The cast of which TV show were described by Dominic Sandbrook as 'working class people bettering themselves and still being tasteless' and by Owen Jones as 'grotesque caricatures of working class life'? According to a 2015 article, the show's popularity has caused the queue for the Sugar Hut in Brentwood to spill 'halfway down the high street at weekends'.

'Oh, no, it isn't!' yells Milbert when you give your answer.

You knead your face in anguish at Milbert's latest outburst. 'Good grief, sir, what's become of me?' you exclaim as you discover your moustache. You are equally startled by your manner of expression as you are by your new-found facial hair. A spacious drawing room materializes around you, rich with the scent of pipe smoke.

# SHERBERT HICKS
# AND THE BLUE GARFUNKEL

*Hints on page 204*

*Answers on page 236*

There is a desperate pounding on the front door. You open it.

'Sherbert Hicks?' demands the young man, who clasps a large goose. 'No, your countenance is too dull and bovine – you must be his associate, Dr Whitsun.'

'A man of astute perceptions,' intones the dryly amused voice of Hicks, who is sitting behind you. 'Come in. Life has been dreary at Loon Warehouse, Flat C, ever since I cleared up the mystery of the missing spanner of Wychwood Manor.'

The man marches past you.

'My name is Che Bilbert Wickles,' he explains. 'I work as a housekeeper at Ixodes Cafe – a tedious job, mostly dealing with country bumpkins who can't decide the simplest thing except by picking bits of paper at random. But last week, this fell out of a van onto the pavement outside.' He indicates the goose. 'I hid the bird and took it home after work, saving it for Christmas. A few days later, I got this note.' He withdraws from his pocket a piece of paper, onto which printed words have been cut out and glued and punctuation drawn on.

> FOR HOUSE KEEPER CHE B. W. TO READ:
>  F Y I :
>  ENTER EN DEN. PUT CEMENT ART ON MAT OR
> BACK OF DE – ICER. MEND LIGHT THAT MAY SURGE.
> UNDRESS. CAN'T CARP OR BE SAD AS MIST; AVER (OR
> RIFF), 'LA, LA! CHER? ER... I AM SHE, AN ELF!'
>  OR WE HAVE WAR.
>  YOURS,
>  QU.

'I've no intention of going anywhere as squalid as the En Den, least of all to fix a light, do a striptease and claim to be Cher!' protests Bilbert Wickles. 'And what's this about "Cement Art"? It baffles the blazes out of me.'

'It could not be simpler,' says Hicks. 'Fixing the light, stripping, talking nonsense – this is merely a distraction so the culprit can escape undetected. As for the identity of "Cement Art", your goose will answer that question.'

Bilbert Wickles gawps at the goose as if half-expecting it to talk. Hicks springs from his chair, snatches the creature and hurls it to the floor. It shatters in a cloud of dust, for it was a painted plaster sculpture all along! From the rubble Hicks extracts a sky-blue cement statuette of Art Garfunkel.

'The Blue Garfunkel,' he declares. 'I've been trying to track this down for years.'

'Rather ugly, isn't it?' you venture.

'Its appearance is irrelevant, Whitsun. It is said that if it is reunited with a cement statuette of Paul Simon, they will sing a version of "Bridge Over Troubled Water" so moving that all the land will weep.'

'Heavens!' bellows Bilbert Wickles.

'Now observe this leaflet from the job centre.' He hands copies to you and Bilbert Wickles. 'It was found by an associate of mine, Nightmog the professional punster, so I had it reproduced by a machine at Fathom Inc., which specializes in such business. The professions listed have been cut out, their parts rearranged to make the threatening note. However, there were certain words that our culprit failed to make from the professions in the leaflet; these he pieced together from words on his own business card. The man who left the note is mentioned in today's newspaper.'

*The leaflet reads:*

1. This Spanish term for a profession was popularized by an opera but is rarely used in Spain, where different terminology is preferred.
2. This term may describe a person who has taken a vow of poverty.

3. Marcus Hanna, who earned both the Gold Lifesaving Medal and the Medal of Honor, served in this profession, as did the father of Grace Darling.

4. Robert Liston was a nineteenth-century exponent of this profession noted for his speed and showmanship; a possibly apocryphal story tells how he inadvertently killed three people, one of whom was his assistant and another was a spectator who died from shock.

5. A person in this profession may work with longstraw, combed wheat reed or water reed.

6. Replacing the last letter of this profession with the letter *e* makes a garment.

7. A 2013 article in *YES!* magazine claimed that under two percent of members of this profession were female, and quoted a woman in this profession as saying, 'Many women are never taught those skill sets when they're young, and so they don't feel comfortable walking onto a construction site to ask for a job, the way many men do getting started.'

8. Jasmine Plummer notably played in this position.

9. 'Give me the _____' bill and I will even set that to music,' said Gioachino Rossini.

10. A man who practises this profession is the title character of the first of Anthony Trollope's *Chronicles of Barsetshire* series.

11. In Greek mythology, Arachne challenges Athena to a contest to see who is better at this profession, while in a Chinese folk tale, a practitioner of this profession is in love with a cowherd.

12. A man who died in 1981 at the age of thirty-six confessed to the shooting of a person in this profession. . .

13. . . .while denying the murder of someone in this profession.

14. Both of the previous professions are sub-categories of this three-word profession.

15. People who served in this profession include Jean de Dinteville and Georges de Selve, who are the title figures of a sixteenth-century painting which shares its name with a twentieth-century novel.

16. Film director Lotte Reiniger, whose work includes the landmark fantasy film *The Adventures of Prince Achmed*, was a pioneer in this profession.

**17.** In Thetford, Norfolk, in 1904, Dr Allan Glaisyer Minns became the first black person in Great Britain to serve in this position.

*Today's newspaper:*

## ANNOUNCEMENTS

Think all concert venues are for oafs? Listen to Mr Jas Quence, owner of The Flamin' Nada, retort. Disregard any anger at Mr Quence's splendid riposte. S Club 7 fans get in free.

Ada Wills wishes to thank Mr Sherbert Hicks for the discovery of the spanner which had gone missing from her home. Her son Quade, of Axel House, also sends his thanks.

Left a locket on the counter at Behave Yourself! nightclub? Contact Quentin Plibb, proprietor.

Lecture at Sadden House by Quincy Strump for those who respond the same way as he does to cabbage.

Rejoin 'Start the Morning with a Quiche', the third series of the popular show, hosted by Art of Quiche owners Ada and Al Querr.

## ROMANCE

You gave me an answer of 'I refuse'? But how? I vowed my love – reciprocate words I write, I beg you! But for you I'm nothing... I am starting to become insane!

You scratch my back? With those fingernails?! Meet at the usual place in your coral dress with that zip! O, all my letters red hot with lust weren't for naught!

Cy: in Melton Mowbray with Mrs Nix, were you? The moment I saw you duck, with that latter day Jezebel, into a sleazy little bar, I realized our marriage was null (also void). Half, HALF, of North Hall is mine now.

I seek your heart – show me the way! I've a Labrador for you. Adorned with a collar of eau de Nil, she truly is the best in Europe. The black coat of the beauteous canine will make you fiercely proud to associate with Sargasso Quoon!

## ADVERTISEMENTS

Zilch Quanty's Alphabet Soup! Try it at Mister She supermarket – you won't regret it!

Hire Xerxes for your office party! A gifted fencer, he has killed thousands!

Have you been injured by a criminal mastermind enacting an awful plot? Visit Quella Onn, the famous 'Warty Lawyer'!

Guilty? Go to Ovid the priest – best confession in town!

66

## Who left the note?

You all head to the En Den. The plan is to watch for the culprit while Bilbert Wickles follows the demands of the note. But his striptease is so hypnotic, his claim to be Cher so electrifyingly outrageous, that you cannot take your eyes off him. When you turn round, the Blue Garfunkel is gone! And there's the culprit, bursting out of the door! You and Hicks give chase (Bilbert Wickles remains, so absorbed in his nonsensical impersonation of Cher that he has entirely forgotten about the Blue Garfunkel), but you crash into a courier holding a tray of plaster sculptures. You tumble to the cobblestones alongside intricate representations of a wrestler, a poet, a mediaeval Arab, a throng of opera singers, and various grotesque and dramatic scenes. Hicks leaps over you like a gazelle and seizes the ruffian by the collar. But the man proves Garfunkel-less, and the exasperated sleuth lets him go.

The courier loads the sculptures into the back of a van.

'Hicks, look at this!' you exclaim. Most of a piece of paper, which had rested beneath one of the sculptures but had been torn loose in the collision, lies at your feet. 'It tells us where they're being delivered.'

'Don't look at it, Whitsun!' yells Hicks, panic in his voice.

'But. . . one of them's going to our flat!'

'Very well! If you wish to ruin the surprise of your Christmas present, consider it ruined.'

You are dumbstruck, both at this unexpected gesture of affection and the fact that Hicks, so adept at seeing into people's souls, had inexplicably thought you would appreciate a sculpture of James K. Polk in a novelty boat. The page reads as follows:

James K. Polk headed down the Po in a boat that resembles a swan, to Loon Warehouse, Flat C

A Christmas goose, to the "Warty Lawyer"

The cast of the Ring cycle, to Sadden House

Alfred, Lord Tennyson, to cousin QW at Axel House

Lady Gaga, who shows she can beat Pol Pot and Osama bin Laden at chess, to Cy Quolloph of North Hall

P. D. James telling a joke at a hen party, to Sargasso Quoon

"Rowdy" Roddy Piper, to Z. Quanty at the Alphabet Soup factory (who yells, "Basket Case!" at passers-by who sport purple polka dots)

'I was thinking,' you suggest, 'that our culprit hid the Garfunkel in one of those sculptures so it could be delivered to his accomplice.'

Hicks snatches the note. 'You may be right, Whitsun. Intriguing. . . one word of each of these descriptions pays tribute to a certain ditty. But what we need is the odd one out – which is written on the missing part of the note.'

'Then all hope's lost, Hicks!'

'*Au contraire.* There are two sides to every piece of paper.' He turns the page around; on the other side is written:

1. Of all the US presidents up to and including Joe Biden, who is the only one whose full name contains a letter of the alphabet not found within the name of any of the fifty current US states?

2. Which words fill the blank space in this extract from Dr. Seuss's *The Lorax*? 'Unless _____ cares a whole awful lot, nothing is going to get better. It's not.' The missing words

form the title of a song which prompted a review on the music website *Pitchfork* to conclude, 'Sometimes, pop music can still break your heart.'

3. A book with the subtitle *A novel in monthly instalments with recipes, romances and home remedies* is known in English by what title? The title is a phrase used to mean 'at boiling point', referring to the required temperature for an ingredient of a sweet drink.

4. A woman born Maria Salomea Skłodowska became better known by which forename and surname, which are spelt identically to each other except for their first two letters?

5. Which politician, born in Alabama in 1954, has a first name derived from a musical term meaning 'with sweetness' in Italian? A space is removed and a *c* is replaced by an *e* to change the musical term into the first name (though please include the politician's surname in your answer as well).

6. Which four French words followed *Bake Off* to complete the title of a spin-off of *The Great British Bake Off* which was later renamed *Bake Off: The Professionals*? The first and fourth words are the same.

7. Which tennis player won nine Grand Slams, eight of which she won while still a teenager? Her surname is a palindrome as it is usually written in English, though it is not palindromic as it appears in Cyrillic or Hungarian.

'Observe, Whitsun. These questions indicate directions to the drop-off point for the sculpture containing the Garfunkel. Unfortunately, these too are incomplete – and since I suspect our driver will take a circuitous route, which may even involve disappearing off one side of this map I have drawn of our town and re-emerging from another—'

'We'll never know the final destination!'

'Blithering nonsense. People leave all kinds of clues without meaning to. One must look for what is omitted. Look at the map, which shows not only streets and buildings but the locations of my associates. You may see what I mean.'

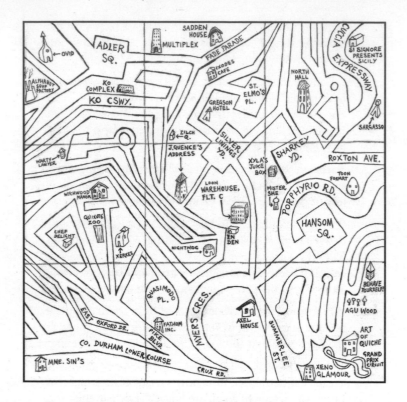

## To which building is the sculpture being taken?

㊼

You race to this building, for there's no time to lose! As you ascend the stairs, a recording performed in a Mexican folk style drifts towards you. 'Que sera, sera. . .' croons the voice, 'Que sera, sera. . .'

'Curses, we're too late!' expostulates Hicks. 'The accomplice has been drugged – in four different ways!'

He pauses, waiting for you to ask how on earth he could possibly know this, but you feel a sudden urge not to give him the satisfaction. He continues with some disgruntlement, '"Sera" is the plural of "serum" – and we heard the word "sera" four times during that recording! Only one man could be responsible for such fiendishness: my arch enemy, Professor Mariachi! He is the most fearsome criminal in town. Once I caught up with him on

East Oxford Drive and tried to placate him with gifts, but he paid them no heed, his countenance cold and hostile, and now he and I are locked in a game of wits, delicately placing our pieces on the board till one of us makes the killer blow.'

You burst into a room, whose inhabitant is slumped unconscious in a corner. Four empty vials are scattered on the floor, alongside a shattered plaster bust and a copy of today's newspaper, open at the same page Hicks showed you. These notes are written in the margin:

Each serum wears off as soon as a dose of the next serum is given. Serum 1 is a simple obedience serum; those who take it will respond to tasks you set them with no attempt to deceive.

Serum 2: Anguilla, Montserrat and Tristan da Cunha are examples of BOTs; what does the letter O stand for in this acronym?

Serum 3: Which three-word phrase (whose first and third word both have the same number of letters and begin with the same letter) fills the blank space in this extract from the BBC's editorial guidelines: 'Offering a _____ to those who are the subject of significant criticism or allegations of wrongdoing is a fairness obligation under the Ofcom Broadcasting Code'? If the second word is replaced by 'to', it becomes the title of a defunct Channel 4 TV show, a 1987 episode of which saw a young Simon Cowell complain that a TV debate about sex was 'boring'.

Serum 4: Which two words follow *A Marriage* to complete the title of a Victorian novel which is thought to have been the first English-language novel to openly portray a sexual relationship between two men? These words also complete the tagline from the film *Cool Runnings*: 'One dream. Four Jamaicans. Twenty. . .'

'Whoever sold Mariachi these sera,' muses Hicks, 'has explained the effects of numbers 2, 3 and 4 by directing him to today's newspaper.'

**What is the hidden message describing the effect of Serum 2?** ㉜
**What is the hidden message describing the effect of Serum 3?** ㉜
**What is the hidden message describing the effect of Serum 4?** ㉜

'And look!' exclaims Hicks. At the bottom of the newspaper Professor Mariachi has written this:

TWO ASSIGNMENTS:

1. SI SIGNORE PRESENTS SICILY – WHERE? FIND THE ROAD ON THE HICKS DRAWING PORTRAYING LOTS OF THOROUGHFARES WITHIN THE TOWN.

2. PROFICIENT SWORDPLAY GIVING RISE TO MASSES OF SLAUGHTER IS A CERTAIN INDIVIDUAL'S JOB – FIND HIM.

Steps of the plan to find the Blue Simon:

A. Give the accomplice Serum 4 and set Assignment 2. Note down the associate of Hicks the accomplice names.

B. Set Assignment 1. (Serum 4 should still be working.) Note down the building the accomplice names.

C. Give the accomplice Serum 2. Demand that the accomplice repeat the answer to step *a*. Note down the building which fits this description.

D. Give the accomplice Serum 1. Set assignment 2. Note down the associate of Hicks the accomplice names.

E. Give the accomplice Serum 2. Demand that the accomplice repeat the previous answer. Note down the building associated with these.

F. Give the accomplice Serum 3. Set assignment 1. Note down the road the accomplice names.

G. Set assignment 2. (Serum 3 should still be working.) Note down the associate of Hicks the accomplice names.

H. Give the accomplice Serum 1. Set assignment 1. Note down the road the accomplice names.*

• • • • • • • • • • • • • • • • • • • • • • • • • • • • • • • • • • • • • • • • • • • • • • • •

* You will gain no points for working out the individual steps of the plan to find the Blue Simon, but they will help you identify which building to head for now.

'We can work out the answers, Whitsun,' muses Hicks, 'but how will this help find the location of the Blue Simon? Ah, but of course!' His keen eyes narrow. 'If we take the first of the first, the second of the second and so on. . . the game of wits is played out! And the Blue Simon will be found in the very place which represents the winning move!'

**Which building must you head for now?** ㊿③

You hurry to the building. As you open the door, an ear-piercing, all-consuming sound fills the air. Your eyes begin to well up with tears. Somewhere unseen, the Blue Simon and the Blue Garfunkel have been reunited, for 'Bridge Over Troubled Water' is playing. And in the middle of the room, dry-eyed and smirking, is Professor Mariachi himself!

'Hicks and Whitsun. How delightful to have your company at my little. . . premiere,' he sneers coolly.

'What?'

'I said, "Hicks and Whitsun"—'

'WHAT?'

'Hicks and Whitsun!'

'WE CAN'T HEAR YOU OVER THE SOUND OF THE MUSIC!'

'HICKS AND WHITSUN!' roars Mariachi, purple in the face. 'HOW DELIGHTFUL TO HAVE YOUR COMPANY AT MY LITTLE PREMIERE! THOSE OTHER TWO CRIMINALS JUST WANTED TO COLLECT THE TEARS OF THE RICH AND FAMOUS, BUT I HAVE A FAR MORE FIENDISH PLAN! I'LL LET THIS SONG PLAY ON REPEAT FOR WEEKS UNTIL THE WHOLE COUNTRY BATHES IN A FLOOD OF TEARS, RUINING ALL THE MUSICAL INSTRUMENTS AND ELECTRICAL EQUIPMENT IN THE LAND! BY THE TIME I STOP THE SONG, EVERYONE WILL BE SO TIRED OF "BRIDGE OVER TROUBLED WATER" THAT THEY'LL FLOCK TO LISTEN TO THE ONLY OTHER MUSIC AVAILABLE – MY COMPILATION OF TRADITIONAL MEXICAN SONGS, WHICH I KEEP IN A WATERPROOF VAULT!'

'WE'RE GOING TO DESTROY THOSE SILLY SIMON AND GARFUNKEL SCULPTURES!' you bellow.

'YOU'LL NEVER FIND WHICH CONTAINER THEY'RE IN!' shrieks Mariachi. 'IF YOU REACH INTO ANY CONTAINER THAT DOESN'T CONTAIN SIMON AND GARFUNKEL, IT'LL BLOW YOU TO KINGDOM COME!' You glance round the room, which contains a bag, a box, a case, a pot, a boat, a jug, a can, a coffin and a basket. 'POOH-POOH TO YOU, DOOMED SLEUTHS!'

He toots a menacing tune on the trumpet, which clashes horribly with the soaring ballad, and somersaults out of the window. But a note has fallen from his pocket! Through your sobs, you make it out.

*How to remember where the Blue Simon and Garfunkel are:*

*Fill in both blanks in the following sequences, with one point per blank space filled, so that each question is out of two points:*

1. *Colo, _____, Dela, Flo, Geo, Ha, _____, Illi*

2. *_____, headed, Pot, _____, D.*

3. *_____. . . : carry to excess or cook for too long; . . ._____: portray or serve as a symbol of; Uma. . .: taste; . . .mine: lack of food; Al. . . too; . . .goon: body of water*

4. *_____ (precedes 'day' to mean a special and memorable day); _____ (name of an organization, consisting of two words beginning with the same letter, formed in 1795 and named in honour of King William III); Fever (illness caused by flavivirus transmitted by infected mosquitoes); Bay (city which is home to the first Super Bowl champions); Nile (river whose source is at Lake Tana, Ethiopia); Girls (band who released 'Closer to Fine'); Chachki (RuPaul's Drag Race champion)*

*Take all the first, then all the second.*

*Apply this to the list.*

Despite Hicks's reputation as cold and sardonic, the music has reduced him to uncontrollable blubbering. It's up to you to save the country from Mariachi's monstrous scheme!

**In which container are the sculpted Simon and Garfunkel?**

# WINTERLUDE 6

*Answers on page 240*

Letter by letter, the words fade from Mariachi's note. 'Bridge Over Troubled Water' slows to a dirge of distorted mooing. You open the container as the room subsides into blackness, and beams of sparkling light gush out and assemble themselves into the form of Milbert. As your moustache detaches itself and bursts into a thousand tiny moustaches, which dance through the darkness and chorus a squeaky, indecipherable song, Milbert asks:

1.  What first name is shared by a *Coronation Street* character from the 1960s who reappeared in 2008 and an obsessed fan of Alan Partridge, whom Partridge calls a 'mentalist'? It is the nickname of the writer of the TV series *Cardiac Arrest*, which was inspired by the writer's experiences as a junior doctor.

2.  Which word is found in a two-word phrase meaning either 'widely distributed missive' or 'O', as well as in phrases denoting the A406 and A205?

3.  Which two initials may refer to a man known for calling for 'clear blue water', who was surprisingly defeated by Stephen Twigg, as well as being initials by which he could no longer describe himself in the wake of his defeat by Stephen Twigg?

4.  Which four-letter preposition becomes a word meaning the same thing if two letters are added to the end of it and becomes a polyhedron if three letters are added to the beginning of it?

5.  Which word may refer to, for instance, a South Korean Netflix series featuring zombies, a British TV series centred on a solicitor, or, for instance, Fungi?

6. Mountains, pretentious, beautiful and elaborate may all be considered opposites of which word?

7. Which word, the surname of a singer-songwriter, may refer to the location of prisoners in an allegory by Plato, and is spelt identically to a Latin word which begins a two-word message found at the House of the Tragic Poet in Pompeii?

8. By taking words which may follow each of these answers to make new words, names or phrases, you can make the title of which Christmas carol?

You feel a floor pulsating beneath your feet. A thunderous chorus wells up in your ears.

# THE GIFT ON THE THIRTEENTH DAY

*Hints on page 206*

*Answers on page 241*

You are in a cramped flat filled with all manner of birds and people engaged in vigorous activities. Swans swim in the bath and the kitchen sink. The floorboards buckle beneath leaping lords. There's barely room to breathe. But today is the thirteenth day of Christmas. The time of gifts is surely over. Yet, over the relentless racket of hordes of pipers and drummers, you can just make out a hammering on the door. You open it to reveal thirteen demons, who burst past you and begin to wreak all manner of havoc. Left in the doorway is a card headed with the words, 'My true love! Here is a quiz for you to enjoy. If you wish to drive out the demons I have so kind-heartedly given you, these questions will help!' And beneath, the following questions are written:

## ROUND 1

1.  Which flower precedes 'path' to mean 'the way of pleasure, which may lead to Hell or to other terrible consequences' or precedes 'Hill' to make a park separated from Regent's Park and London Zoo by Prince Albert Road?

2.  The director Uwe Boll named as his favourite horror films *The Shining* and a film whose central character has which first name? This name is also the third word of the title of a Simon & Garfunkel album.

3.  The musician and artist E. Jane (also known as MHYSA), who described the Noisettes song 'Iwe' as being among their influences, is from which US state? Its state bird is an oriole in whose honour its most populous city's baseball team is named.

4. While living in London (which was home to one of his favourite artists, Frank Holl), Vincent Van Gogh is thought to have been infatuated with either his _____ or her daughter. Which word, which appears in the title of a Kirsty MacColl album, fills the blank space? This word denotes a profession shared by Sue Matthews, who had sheep pens installed to encourage her patrons to have a drink and a meal while remaining socially distanced (prompting the *Teesdale Mercury* to quip, 'EWE WHAT?'), and *Gogglebox*'s Jenny Newby, who met Lee Riley when he was a regular at the Crown Inn, a village pub near Hull.

5. The star of which film was described by an RTÉ headline as being 'in awe' of its effect, quoting her as saying, 'It really has sort of become a film for the generation, I think'? The title character, Christine McPherson, uses a name which was also the nickname of an American who had the crowd sing along to 'Puff, the Magic Dragon' at a dinner for UN Secretary-General U Thant.

6. Somebody with what on their feet (which have been caused by repeated friction) may be able to traverse rough land with less pain? This plural noun contains, spelt backwards, the name of a general who rose to power after a civil war.

### ROUND 2

1. The Hunter process and the Kroll process are used to extract which element, which is named after figures in Greek mythology and shares its name with a song by David Guetta featuring Sia?

2. 'Excuse me, _____ – what do you know about rough areas?' demanded the *Guardian* in response to a programme presented by the author of *Lionel Asbo*, who claimed that multiculturalism was failing, especially in 'rough areas'. The article concluded that this author's political views were becoming increasingly reminiscent of those of his father in his old age. Which words (a two-letter title followed by a surname) fill in the blank space?

3. In 1604, the Polish alchemist Michael Sendivogius used the term 'food of life' apparently to refer to which substance? Carl Wilhelm Scheele described this substance as 'fire air', Joseph Priestley called it 'dephlogisticated air' and Antoine Lavoisier gave it the name we know it by now, though he also referred to it as 'vital air'.

4. Which surname fills in the blank in this sequence: 1970: Müller; 1974: _____; 1978: Kempes; 1982: Rossi? This surname is also a Latin word which follows 'sensu' to make an expression meaning 'in the broad sense'.

5. Four chemical elements begin with a letter of the alphabet which no other element begins with: krypton, uranium, vanadium and which other?

6. What is the name of the capital of Colombia's Bolívar Department, which is named after a city in Murcia, Spain, which was itself named after an ancient city in what is now Tunisia?

7. Which word is missing from the name of the Brotherhood of Sleeping Car _____, the first labour union led by African-Americans to be affiliated with the American Federation of Labor, which is also missing from the name of the Society for the Prevention of Calling Sleeping Car _____ 'George' (founded in reaction to members of this profession being frequently addressed as 'George' as a reference to George Pullman)? This word may also mean 'dark brown beers'.

8. The American Film Institute's *100 Years. . . 100 Movie Quotes* contains lines from *Funny Girl*, the 1983 version of *Scarface*, and *Jerry Maguire*, all of which include which word?

### ROUND 3

1. Which word denotes a small cake eaten in Australia or New Zealand, similar to a financier? The word is borrowed from French, though in French it refers to a sausage roll. Replacing the letter *a* in this word with a different vowel

makes a word whose French equivalent is found within an answer to the previous round.

2. Removing the middle letter from the name of which constellation gives you the name of a god whose Roman counterpart has a planet named after him?

3. Meanings of which word include 'narrative poem or ballad', 'not ecclesiastical' and 'set down'?

4. Which Colombian city is also the stage name of a Colombian musician who is part of a pop duo alongside his brother 'El Dandee'? This name is also the first four letters of a US state, which is used as a nickname for the state (though this nickname is rarely used by locals).

5. Words meaning 'deities', 'imaginary scary creatures' and 'small rodents' can all precede the same two words and follow which word to make the names of, respectively, a film set in Algeria, an Icelandic band and a twentieth-century novella?

6. 'The blaze of crimson light from the tube told its own story and was a sight to dwell upon and never forget,' remarked the co-discoverer of which element, which has the shortest name of any of the six naturally occurring noble gases?

7. The name of which tool used for castrating livestock can be formed by inserting three letters (which may follow names of cinematographers in film credits) into a word meaning 'a program which allows software designed for one computer to be run on an entirely different computer' or, more generally, 'someone or something that imitates'?

8. The ninth Stoke Mandeville games, which are considered the first official Paralympic Games, were held in which city? This city contains the Quirinal Palace.

1. Which word follows *Les pêcheurs de* to complete the title of an opera by Georges Bizet? If one letter is removed from this word, it becomes the surname of a man who served as both Prime Minister and President of Israel.

2. An actor born Mark Sinclair first adopted his stage name while working as a bouncer. What is his stage forename, which is the first syllable of his mother's married surname – a surname which is also the name of a saint after whom a country's largest island is named?

3. Which two-letter word both precedes and succeeds *Shanti* to complete the title of a Bollywood film? This word precedes *mani padme hum* to make a mantra.

4. Which word may precede 'ship' to make a type of ship, 'pigeon' to make an extinct species, or '57' to make the title of an action film?

5. Which two letters, the initials of the composer of the 1829 opera *William Tell*, distinguish the names of two keys on a computer keyboard which are often found either side of the spacebar?

6. What is the shortened given name of the founder of the Kyokushin style of karate who was born with the name Choi Yeong-Eui, as well as being the first word of the title of a song by Jorge Ben which became Sérgio Mendes's signature song? If three letters are added to the end of the previous answer and three different letters are added to the end of this answer, they combine to make a word which could describe Judit Polgár or Fabiano Caruana.

7. Which rare five-letter word means 'remove from a metal container'? An anagram of this word can be followed by the previous answer with an accent above one of its letters to form a phrase which might be uttered by a Spanish-speaking raven.

8. Which word, which begins the title of a song whose narrator compares his love life to betting on a horse which narrowly loses, can be followed by two letters to make a

word meaning 'resembling or related to sexually explicit material'? If the same two letters follow the previous answer, it makes a word meaning 'disturbingly strange'.

## ROUND 5

1. Meanings of which word include 'make or shape' and 'move forwards'? It is also a synonym of the nickname of a character played by James Corden who impregnates another answer in this round.

2. Josh Gad, who voices Olaf in *Frozen*, also appeared in a Broadway musical whose title ends in which word and whose songs were co-written by Robert Lopez, who would go on to co-write *Frozen*'s songs? Gad stated that 'a few people – a dozen' had told him they had been so moved by the show that they adopted the faith of the musical's protagonists.

3. Which name precedes 'Mike' to make a nuclear test which destroyed the island of Elugelab and, when preceded by a certain six-letter word, makes a name shared by a comic-book character and a 1992 erotic thriller film?

4. *Discourses Concerning Government, Poems and Ballads* and *Incredible Adventures* are works by authors who share which forename, which is also the name shared by two fictional characters, one of whom is a mouse whose intelligence is increased through an experimental surgical procedure and the other escapes social engagements by claiming he must visit an invalid named Bunbury?

5. What is the second word of a three-word term for a plot device? The first two words of this term are the name of a video game which has a prequel entitled *Human Revolution* and the last two words of this term are the name of a film in which Alicia Vikander plays a robot.

6. Which short first name is shared by a man who stood for election in Sedgefield against Tony Blair after his son was killed in the Iraq War and an actor who starred as a driver in a sitcom which ran from 1969 to 1973? It

precedes *Strikes Back* to complete the name of an album
by a musician formerly known by this name.

7. What is the five-letter stage forename of a singer-songwriter
   whose songs include 'i hope ur miserable until ur dead'
   and 'la di die'?

8. Which word, defined by Collins Dictionary as 'an organic
   compound used to make allyl alcohol', can be formed by
   taking a word found in the titles of a Jonathan Swift essay
   satirically calling for impoverished Irish parents to sell their
   children as food and a film in which Robert Redford plays
   a character who, in the novel it is based on, was depicted
   as a wealthy Arab named Ibrahim, and replacing the
   fifth, sixth and seventh letters with the surname of Brian,
   a former member of Roxy Music whose albums include
   *Music for Airports*?

### DRIVING OUT THE DEMONS:

The dancing ladies that were given to you at Christmas are still
cavorting through your flat. Lady Mary, Lady Adelaide, Lady
Isabella and Lady Henrietta are the wildest of them all, crowing
that they have abandoned the stuffy propriety of the aristocracy.
Remove four words found in Round 1's questions from Round 1's
answers and read the resulting words in reverse order to find out
**how to drive one of these ladies to such indignation** that she
hurls a demon through the window.  ㉑

The sound of one of your previous gifts is enough to alarm one
of the more skittish demons into leaving. **This sound** is notably
missing from Round 1's answers.  ㉑

In the same way that 'O' could be considered missing from
Round 1's questions, find words missing from three other sets of
four non-consecutive words in Round 1's questions, which can be
pieced together to make the name of **this film**, which will terrify
a demon into leaving.  ㉑

Threaten a demon by claiming to be as strong as **these two
famous rivals**; transferring the first letter of one answer to the
beginning of the previous answer produces two surnames used

by the first, while the name of the second rhymes with two consecutive answers. (Separate your two answers with a semi-colon.) Ⓐ

The first letters of the answers in one round spell out **the profession** of someone you must hire to train your turtle doves to drive out a demon (although this person bitterly complains that she is not used to working with doves). Ⓐ

One demon has woven an especially horrifying trail of destruction through your flat. Treat the demon with **this** – which can be found by removing the final letter from odd-numbered answers in the same round – which it finds so baffling that it flees. Ⓑ

Entice a demon out of your door by promising it a trip to **this imaginary realm**. This realm's name is an anagram of two answers in the same round, and this realm's (equally imaginary) inhabitants rhyme with the answer found between them. Ⓑ

Five answers in this quiz, when letters are inserted into them, become names of male characters in different works by the same author. These letters or strings of letters, arranged in alphabetical order (but without anagramming), spell out a creature which one demon fears above all things; use **this creature** to drive the demon out. Ⓑ

Find an answer which contains two other answers within it. Remove these two answers and, in their place, insert the symbols of four other answers (in reverse alphabetical order) to make **the profession** of a person you invite to your flat. A demon, fearing for its life, will flee down the fire escape. Ⓑ

Two answers in the same round, which have the same number of letters, have five letters in common. When those five letters are removed from the later answer, the remaining letters spell out the stage surname of a man who notably sang of an answer in the previous round. Follow this stage surname with a three-letter word found within the longest answer in a round, which would also be found within an answer in the same round if it contained a full name rather than a title and a surname. You have made the name of a movement. Show the work of **this leading figure in the movement**, who lived from 1928 to 1987, to one demon to make it retreat to contemplate the work more deeply. Ⓑ

Two answers in the same round are homophones of things with something in common. Multiply them. Remove the first two letters from an answer so that it has the same number of letters as the answer before and after it, then follow this with the closest answer before it which has the same number of letters as it originally had (before you removed the first two). **These** are what you must unleash to drive out a demon. ㉜

Find a word which is not an answer in this quiz but which, judging by the pattern established in one round, should be. Utter **this monosyllabic word** to make one demon acutely aware of its isolation in the world; it will retire to ponder this. ㊷

The fiercest and most malevolent of the thirteen demons remains. The three ways of driving out demons which relate to Round 1 form the first group. The rest of the answers can be sorted into three more groups, such that one can start at the first group, move through the second, the third, the fourth, the third, the second and back to the first to make something associated with certain characters. **Which groups should the ways of driving out demons fit into?** ㊷

Certain answers to this quiz share some of their letters with these characters; take their other letters. Follow this with a final letter. One answer in this quiz comes before another in the same language; if you take their English equivalents and add this letter, it would mean, 'something valuable offered to someone unappreciative'. You have spelt out **these members of a profession**, which you must hire if you have any hope of eliminating the final demon! ㊷

# WINTERLUDE 7

*Answers on page 244*

Of the thirteen demons, the final one was the most fearsome. Now it slinks away with a wretched howl, as the room around you melts like Salvador Dalí's clocks and drips into the void. 'We're well on our way!' enthuses Milbert, whose disembodied head has appeared atop a floating cushion, which gradually stretches down and becomes the rest of his body. 'Who knows, I might just get my wings after all. Oh Jim, I hope I can save you!' You want to say, 'But what about *me*?' but you suspect that Milbert will airily reply as if no-one as unimportant as you could possibly matter, even to yourself. And it's hardly as if you have a choice but to do what Milbert says, no matter what happens. Even if he let you refuse to go to the next dimension, you'd just be sitting here in the void twiddling your thumbs and wondering if you can see any patterns in the blackness. So you just let him ask you the following questions:

1. Which first name is shared in the names of two acts who had UK Christmas number one singles twenty-six years apart, the first of which was an instrumental? In the name of the group which released the second single, the person with this first name did not perform on the song, having been (reputedly) decapitated long before the date of the recording.

2. According to the Norwegian parasitologist Odd Halvorsen, a parasitic infection of the respiratory system is most likely responsible for which character's distinctive appearance?

3. Who, upon being elected to a prestigious new job in 2006, sang a version of 'Santa Claus Is Coming to Town' at a gala, inserting his own name in place of 'Santa Claus'?

4. What do the following have in common: the drag performer Anthony Taylor, the comic-book character Mari McCabe, the quizzer Jenny Ryan and one of Father Christmas's reindeer?

5. The aromatic resin extracted from plants of the genus *Commiphora* is commonly known by which five-letter name?

6. Which Nobel laureate was credited by the United States Golf Association with inventing the sport of snow golf and wrote the first ever Royal Christmas Message, which was broadcast by George V?

7. The main character of which seasonal film is depicted passing by London shops called Micklewhite's and Statler and Waldorf?

8. 'Christmas Eve, and twelve of the clock,' begins a Thomas Hardy poem titled 'The *what*'? The missing word is the plural of a type of animal which Hardy describes as kneeling in front of the baby Jesus, and a city which houses the Pitt Rivers Museum was built on the site of a river crossing for such animals.

You have shrunk. You are enveloped in a frilly dress and your hair is arranged into neat little pigtails.

# THE NUT-KRAKEN

*Hints on page 207*

*Answers on page 245*

Tonight Mother has let you stay up late. Your brother had played too roughly with your Kraken-shaped nutcracker – a gift from your godfather Dieselmotor, who somehow bears an unmistakable resemblance to it, although it is impossible to pinpoint any feature which the two of them share. Mother took the boy to bed.

Dieselmotor, with a sphinxlike smile, leaves the room. The moment he shuts the door, the Nut-Kraken begins to whisper, giving you a terrible fright. Its voice is high-pitched and skittish. 'A creature lurks beneath the playroom, Miss Bettina. She is a seven-headed meerkat, bent on causing the most beastly havoc. We must line up our troops, Miss Bettina, to defeat her!'

As if on cue, a fearsome scrabbling and squealing is heard beneath the room's tiles. The Nut-Kraken wriggles from your grasp, hissing at the surrounding toys and objects, 'You, figurine of a playwright, to square g1! Not so lazily now – have you no consideration for my feelings? You, make-up bag, to k2! Young Batman, to f3 immediately! Copy of *Atonement* with the letters *ment* torn off, to l1! Pair of apes, to a7!'

The toys and assorted objects in the playroom shuffle into position at the Nut-Kraken's command. 'Listen, my dears, I want you all ears!' it announces, clapping four of its tentacles together. 'Six of the items in the playroom will make six moves – or, if they cannot make as many as six, as many as they can before they reach the edge! The moves will be coordinated, everyone making their first move at the same time, their second move at the same time, their third move at the same time – well, *surely* you understand by now. One of the items moves right. A second jumps over items which follow "jump the" to make idioms; it begins by moving in the direction of the closest of those items to it and continues in the same direction. A third starts by moving diagonally up and right, but turns 90° to the right under certain circumstances. A fourth can only move onto tiles which share a particular characteristic. The fifth and sixth items move diagonally down and right and diagonally down and left respectively – you'll be able to identify those two soon, Miss Bettina. The little swirly things are teleporters – that is to say, my dear, that if you go in one of them, you will come straight out of the other one, moving in the same direction. So, if you moved from b5 to b6, your next move would take you from m1 to m2. The six moving items will only stop when their six moves are up, or when they bump into the edge of the room!'

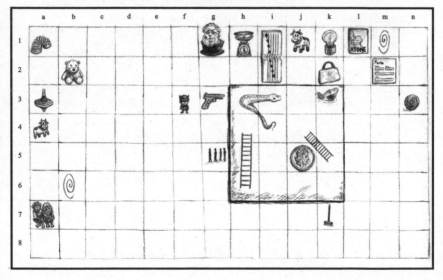

'Now we must work out which pieces move where. Here's a letter from Dieselmotor's writing-desk! What you have to do is take the first letter of the first word of the first line, the first letter of the second word of the second line, the first letter of – well, *surely* you understand by now – until you've spelt out the name of the item which moves diagonally down and right. Then you take the first letter of the last word of the first line, the first letter of the penultimate word of the second line, and so on and so forth, until you've spelt out the name of the item which moves diagonally down and left. A simple task, Miss Bettina!' The letter reads:

---

*You are proficient enough on the piano, my lovely, to play Chop-In at the Palladium during a concert satirizing Glenn Gould? Refine your artistry! Even The fauna of a European city is more majestic than new artifices, such as your candle-Sticks, which may perhaps be seen as too meaningless for an up-Holder of great beauty. One thinks of nature, calmly and jovially. Isn't this awful, to rid Bel-Grade of this nature? You'll easily escape shock and amazement if I say, 'Remember! Have you helped yourself to a bass while partaking in a break-Fast of fish? I know that you were reportedly planning to do such a thing soon.'*

---

'Yaopoebw and Caamiaar?' you say (with some difficulty). 'But Nut-Kraken, I keep no such horribly named toys in my playroom! Even my brother draws the line at Mega-Smash-Demon.'

'Oh, that wretched meerkat!' wails the Nut-Kraken, wringing its tentacles. 'She's rearranged the letter so that the lines appear in the wrong order. She's always sneaking in and messing things about! Oh, my poor nerves. This isn't what Dieselmotor was *really* writing about. Why, he'd been accusing the man he was writing to of burglary, describing his musical skill (and the prospect of him improving it) in unflattering terms, praising the beauty of an object the man owns but claiming that it is still inferior to nature and, finally, asserting that the man wants to remove certain creatures from a European city. *Now*, dear Miss Bettina, **which item in the playroom moves diagonally down and right** and **which one moves diagonally down and left**? ㉜

'Now, my dear,' continues the Nut-Kraken, 'here is a crossword for you. I do hope you like crosswords. I'm afraid that all the dainty little numbers are in a muddle, not at all how I remember them, so let's pay the numbers no attention and give you the clues in order as you'd expect, with the first two across clues filling the five-letter gap and the six-letter gap in the top row respectively, and so on and so forth. This will help us continue our battle plan.'

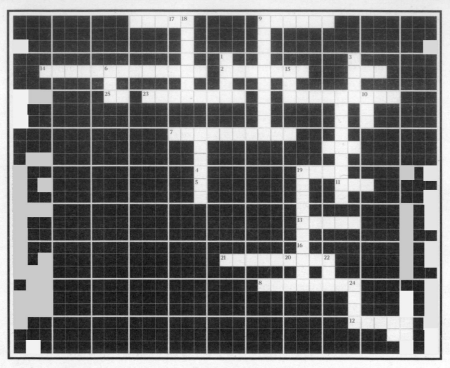

ACROSS:

A. Buster Douglas's defeat of Mike Tyson in 1990 was named *What* of the Year by *The Ring* magazine? The word I'm looking for may also mean 'distress' or 'knock over', as well as being used in cryptic crosswords to indicate an anagram.

B. Which two words fill in the blank space in this extract from a speech by Martin Luther King, Jr., given the day before his assassination: 'I've seen the Promised Land. I _____ get there with you'? According to *The Cambridge History of the English Language*, a contraction of these two words (in which a space is removed and one letter is replaced by an apostrophe) has 'moved from colloquial normality to great rarity in the course of the twentieth century'.

C. Which two words, which both end in the same two letters, precede 'governance institution' to make a phrase with the acronym ILGI? They together form an anagram of 'frolic on llama'.

D. Which word denotes fruits also known as alligator strawber-ries? If the letters of this word (with a space added after the first two letters) are inserted into the name of a US state, it becomes a phrase meaning 'for the most part, a dairy product'.

E. Which word meaning 'anger' is spelt identically to the Latin for 'to go' and begins the name of a European country?

F. What is the title of a 1927 film which defines its title as 'that quality possessed by some which draws all others with its magnetic force'? The film provided its star, Clara Bow, with her nickname.

G. Which two words, which are both the same length and begin with the same two letters, fill the blank space in this quotation from Shakespeare's *Henry VI, Part III*: 'See the minutes, how they run, / How _____ the hour full complete'?

H. Also called an evaporimeter, what is the name of an instrument which measures the rate of evaporation of water? The first three letters of this word are an acronym for a type of machine, the first of which in the UK was opened in Enfield, with *On the Buses* star Reg Varney its inaugural user.

I. Traditional didgeridoos are commonly made from the wood of which genus of trees? An essential oil is extracted from the leaves of several trees in this genus, whose name derives ultimately from Greek words meaning 'well' and 'covered'.

J. Which acronym is shared by Asia's oldest stock exchange and a disease also known as mad cow disease?

K. What name is shared by an island in the Inner Hebrides and a mountain range after which the period between the Triassic and Cretaceous is named?

L. K and Ed Tom Bell are characters portrayed by Tommy Lee Jones in a 1997 film and a 2007 film respectively; which word do the two films share in their titles?

M. The first person to win an acting Oscar for a performance in a foreign language was born with the surname Scicolone (and with a first name which was originally spelt with an *f* rather than a *ph*). What stage surname did she adopt?

N. A digital distribution platform which offers downloadable newspapers, magazines and journals is known as a digital what? The word I'm looking for contains just two vowels and, if its two syllables are swapped round and a space is inserted between them, they become the name of a Hong Kong pro-democracy website which was shut down in 2021 following a police raid.

o. Which two words fill the blank space in this headline from *The Hindu*: 'Karachi priest not allowed to _____ to India'? If the letter *t* is added to the beginning of the second word, it becomes a phrase meaning 'do something one after another in succession'.

p. Which word, which may be a slang term used in skateboarding, skiing or snowboarding, has meanings including 'cut into thin strips' and 'play an instrument (particularly the electric guitar) in a fast, technically proficient style'?

q. A *Star Trek: The Next Generation* character played by Michelle Forbes has what short first name, which may be prefixed to a word meaning 'excessive enthusiasm' or 'a phase of bipolar disorder' to make the name of a country?

DOWN:

a. Siena and Pisa are cities within a region of Italy known in English by what name? The only woman who was subject to a biography in Lytton Strachey's *Eminent Victorians* was born in the capital of this region, which was then a grand duchy.

b. Which two-word term, synonymous with 'ignis fatuus' or 'will-o'-the-wisp', may be spelt as one word to form the title of a Joy Ellis novel featuring Matt Ballard? It can be formed from the surname of another crime writer followed by the word which precedes *Thickens* to give the title of her final completed novel to feature Roderick Alleyn.

c. Which four-letter word, meaning 'anti-aircraft fire' or 'criticism', was originally an abbreviation of the German word *Fliegerabwehrkanone*?

d. 'Building', 'camp', 'web' and 'caravan' can all precede which four-letter word to make words and phrases?

e. Which French word, spelt identically to the surname of Jomo Kenyatta's successor as President of Kenya, is the name of a perfume launched by Miss Piggy and follows 'Pretentious?' to complete the punchline of a joke told in an episode of *Fawlty Towers*?

F. Which word comes between 'eon' and 'period' on the geologic time scale, and is found in secular equivalents of 'Before Christ' and 'Anno Domini'?

G. Which words, which may mean 'changes the position of sloping surface', fill the blank space in this extract from an article in *Men's Health* magazine: 'These total-body _____ up your heart rate while toning you up'? I'm looking for an anagram of 'more vamps'.

H. 2240 pounds, 2000 pounds and approximately 2204.6 pounds are all equivalent to units sharing which three-letter name, which may be distinguished as 'long', 'short' and 'metric' respectively?

I. Which archaic word is found (twice) in an idiom meaning 'when a saviour is required, one appears' as well as being found (once) in the title of a play set in Harry Hope's saloon (an establishment the *New York Post* described as possibly '[t]he most depressing place in American drama')?

J. Which term for a fundraising event in which second-hand items are sold can be formed from the name of William Brown's dog in Richmal Crompton's stories followed by the name of a town in Greater Manchester?

K. Which word for a dung beetle, if an apostrophe is inserted, concludes the name of two awards? Kevin Keegan and Ken Loach were, respectively, the first British people to win these awards twice.

L. Which word begins the names of a jazz band which released the album *Your Queen Is a Reptile*, a D. H. Lawrence novel with the working title *Paul Morel* (after its protagonist) and a TV series which spawned the spin-off *Mayans M.C.*?

M. Plato's *Republic* concludes with the tale of a man known in English by what name, who is presumed dead but returns to recount his experience of the afterlife? This name is spelt identically to the symbol for an element first discovered in Ytterby, Sweden, to the Norwegian word for 'is' and to a pronoun in German.

N. Giovanni Batista Doni is said to have been responsible, in the seventeenth century, for changing the note formerly known as 'ut' to what, apparently renaming the note after himself? This note is sometimes spelt with the letter *h* at the end, but I would like it without the *h* here.

'So,' announces the Nut-Kraken, 'there we are, Miss Bettina! Four of the answers are messages telling you which items move where.'

'I see no messages, Nut-Kraken.'

'But nothing could be simpler, Miss Bettina, you just – oh! Oh, the beast!'

'You look quite pale, dear Nut-Kraken!'

'It's that seven-headed meerkat again, who delights in rearrangement! This is the real crossword—' (it seizes a pen and, with careful tentacles, sketches out a new grid) 'and here are the real clues.'

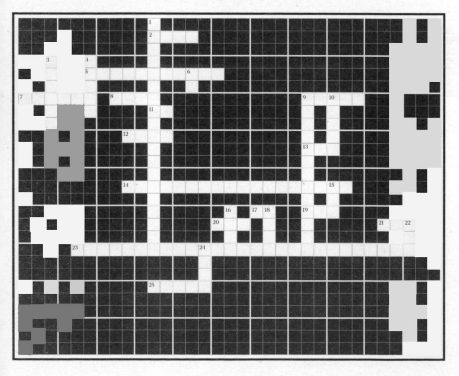

2. Australian birds in the genus *Menura*, which are known for their ability to mimic sounds, derive their name from the supposed resemblance of the male's tail to which instrument, associated with the mythological character Orpheus?

5. The first six letters of which word, meaning 'hearty eater', mean 'long, narrow hole or ditch', while the last six letters of the word are a first name shared by authors who created the fictional seafarers Queequeg and Queeg?

7. The joker card originated in which card game, in which it can serve as the top trump or 'best bower'? It has been speculated that the joker card got its name owing to the similarity between the word 'joker' and the name of this game.

8. What first name was shared by two socialites, one of whom died in a car crash which inspired the Beatles' 'A Day in the Life', while the other finished runner-up in the first series of *I'm a Celebrity. . .Get Me Out of Here!* and underwent surgery after her nasal septum collapsed from cocaine use?

9. Which word concludes both a phrase meaning 'school, college or university that one previously attended' and the title of a mediaeval Latin hymn describing the Virgin Mary's sorrow at Jesus's crucifixion? It may be preceded by 'dura', 'arachnoid' and 'pia' to make the names of the meninges (membranes enveloping the brain and spinal cord).

11. Which word, spelt identically to an abbreviation for a US state, forms the title of Elton John's autobiography, ghostwritten by Alexis Petridis?

12. Which word begins the titles of both a British comedy series whose theme tune spells out its title in Morse code (minus the apostrophes at the beginning of the final two words) and a film containing the line 'Look how she moves. That's just like Jell-O on springs. She must have some sort of built-in motors. I tell you, it's a whole different sex!'

13. Which word may denote a hot, dry summer wind in North India and Pakistan, a card game or a toilet?

17. The ampersand originated as a representation of which Latin word, which is spelt identically to its French equivalent?

19. Which word, meaning 'extend' or 'stick out', precedes 'land' to form the name of a European peninsula?

20. The authors of *The Kitchen God's Wife* and the wordless graphic novel *The Arrival* share which surname? It is also a word whose meanings include 'thrash' and 'convert (animal hide) into leather'.

21. Which Scottish term for a hooligan is also a name shared by characters in *Spider-Man* comics, *A Song of Ice and Fire* and *The Simpsons*, though it is short for a different name in each case?

25. Reinhold Messner, who made the first solo ascent of Mount Everest, Mahmood, who finished runner-up in the 2019 Eurovision Song Contest, and Marcell Jacobs, who won gold in the men's 100 metres at the 2020 Olympics, are all from which country (although Jacobs was born in the USA)? A period of political turmoil in this country, during which a former prime minister was kidnapped and murdered, was known as the 'Years of Lead'.

DOWN:

3. The BBC series *Pinwright's Progress*, of which all episodes are lost, has been described as the first *what* on television? I'm looking for a single-word answer, which is an abbreviation for a two-word term.

4. Meanings of which word include 'colourless, flammable liquid' and 'heavens'? It is the title of a book of the Book of Mormon, which, if the letter *s* is inserted, becomes the title of a book of the Bible.

6. Which word precedes both 'Money' and 'Problems' in the title of a posthumously released Notorious B.I.G. single? This word's two letters also form an abbreviation of a Latin phrase meaning 'method'.

10. What is the name of a particularly densely populated district of Manila as well as a word denoting a circular painting or sculpture?

15. Which abbreviation is used in American English to denote a form of hormone therapy, though it is rarely used in British

English, where the hormone in question begins with a different first letter? This abbreviation is spelt identically to a rare word whose (far more common) opposite means 'unable to move' or 'chemically inactive'.

16. Which substance is found in idioms meaning 'honest and decent person', 'efficient and deserving of one's wages', 'make a painful situation even worse' and 'view something with a suspicion that it may not be entirely true'?

18. Which surname is shared by a politician who served both as Prime Minister of Poland and President of the European Council and a *Rick and Morty* character who is a parody of (and is voiced by) a South African-born entrepreneur and who has long, pointed teeth protruding from his mouth?

22. Which acronym is used in computing to denote either system software formerly used in computers or a type of cyber-attack, depending on whether the middle letter is capitalized or not?

24. Which company's name was inspired partly by a word used in English to address a boy (which is also the nickname of James Caan's character in *The Godfather*) and partly by a Latin word for 'sound'?

'Now!' cries the Nut-Kraken. 'Tell me, dear Bettina: **what are the four answers in the grid that tell you which pieces you must move and how you must move them?** These four answers don't have clues, you know!'

'I've got it, dear Nut-Kraken!' you exclaim. 'Now the items will move and the wicked meerkat will surely be defeated – the playroom will be saved from her havoc!'

'If only it were that easy,' sighs the Nut-Kraken.

'*Easy?*' you expostulate, but your little tentacled companion ignores you.

'If the six items move in the correct way, all at the same time, two of the six will occupy the same square on six occasions. Look at Dieselmotor's letter! It doesn't matter whether you look at the meerkat's rearranged version or the original, for you won't go from one line to the next! For instance, Miss Bettina, if two moving items both occupied i8, you would read 'le partak'; if two moving items both occupied l7, you would read 'to rid Be'. If two moving items both occupied m3, you would read 'ore'. But I am over-explaining, my dear. **What is the final message, which tells you what to move and how, so that the wicked creature's muddles and messes can be undone forever?'**

The meerkat's seven snarling heads burst through the tiles. But you have anticipated the attack, and the terrible creature, horrified by what is hurtling towards her, plunges back beneath the floor. She is never seen or heard from again.

# WINTERLUDE 8

*Answers on page 249*

Your surroundings melt away as vigorous music swells and fades. 'Not too bad, Miss Quincunx,' says Milbert. 'Let's have a Christmas palindrome while you get into your next body.'

'A Christmas *what*?'

'Don't you have that tradition? Of course – silly me! I forgot I created you so that your Christmases lacked jollity. You had "find the nail clippings in the custard", if I'm not mistaken.'

'I *hated* that game. Couldn't you have given me games that didn't involve nail clippings or mothballs or rusty gardening tools?'

'Well, perhaps having one minor character with a happy childhood wouldn't have made a difference to Jim – he'd still have realized how awful life would have been if he'd never been born. But don't worry, Miss Quincunx, if I get him out of there, he'll never have to meet anyone with such a grisly past again! I'm going to take him to a dimension with sand and sunshine, and maybe I can sit next to him and we'll share a pineapple rum punch!' He stifles an excited giggle, then continues, 'Anyway, the answers to this round – if spaces, punctuation and capitalization are disregarded – collectively form a giant palindrome, that is to say, a string of letters which reads the same forwards and backwards.'

1. Which word fills the blank in the title of the Dutch Christmas carol 'O Kerstnacht, Schoner Dan _____ Dagen', which is spelt identically to the word that fills the blank space in the title of the French Christmas carol 'Cantique _____ Noël'?

2. Which word follows 'The Christmas' to complete the title of a historical romance story by Mary Jo Putney? The title

refers not to a delicacy but to a woman who is offered money to sleep with a nobleman.

3. Which two words (followed by a comma) precede 'Santa' to form the headline of a *USA Today* article about people engaging in a water sport while dressed as Father Christmas to raise money for a cancer charity?

4. The 1997 made-for-TV film *On the 2nd Day of Christmas*, described by the online magazine *Bustle* as 'the best Christmas movie ever', stars which American actor as the male lead? His name rhymes with that of a character who possesses (among other features) 'a poisonous wart at the end of his nose'.

5. Which character in Disney's *Frozen* is the title character of two spin-offs, one of which is a short film where he has a *Frozen Adventure* at Christmastime and the other is a series in which he retells classic Disney stories?

6. In Charles Dickens's *A Christmas Carol*, the Ghost of Christmas Present is described as 'clothed in one simple green robe, or mantle, bordered with white' what? The word I'm looking for is also the name of an ethnic group whose name makes up the second half of a region of Sudan which they inhabit.

7. What is the single-word name of the demonic, goat-like figure in Central European folklore who is said to punish naughty children at Christmas? It also forms the title of a 2015 horror film.

8. Which word fills both blank spaces in this quotation from the villainous Mr Potter in *It's a Wonderful Life*: 'You once called me a warped, _____ old man. What are you but a warped, _____ young man?'

Your body remains childlike, though your pigtails have evaporated. In front of you is a window, beyond which a field of wheat stretches out.

# THE CROW MAN

*Hints on page 208*

*Answers on page 250*

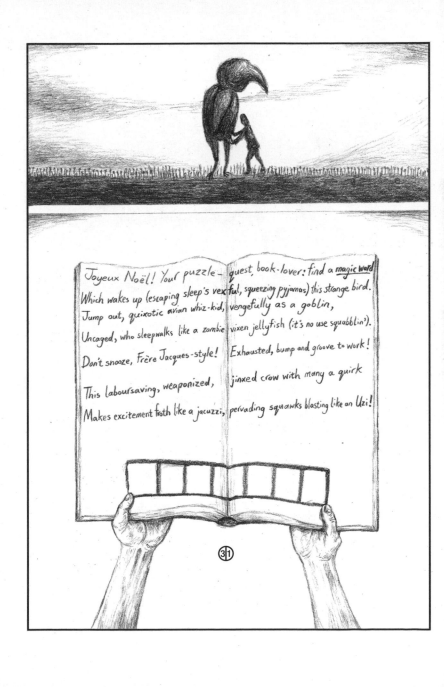

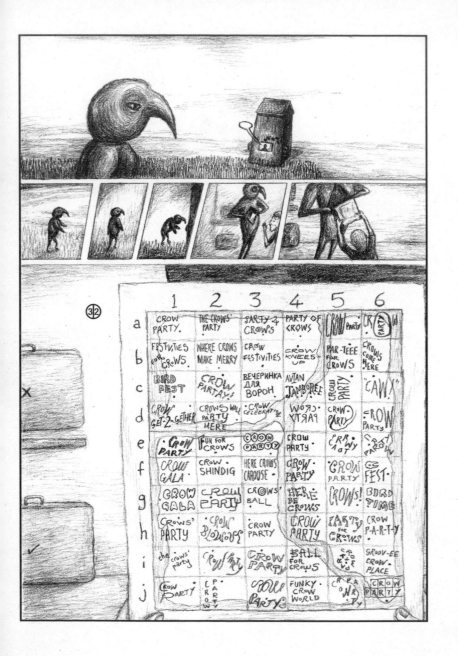

THE DANCE IS OVER.

THE WAR RE-ENACTMENT BEGINS.

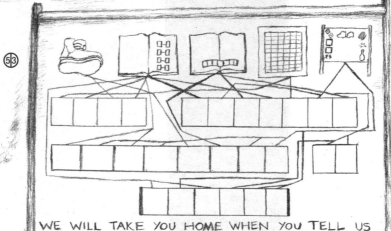

WE WILL TAKE YOU HOME WHEN YOU TELL US WHICH WAR WE ARE RE-ENACTING.

# WINTERLUDE 9

*Answers on page 251*

'Answer us!' each rifle seems to roar, and as you open your mouth to speak, the snow and the sky blend into an all-encompassing blanket of white. The angel appears. 'Oh, Milbert, that was *harrowing*.'

'The festive season can be harrowing, Miss Quincunx,' he sighs. 'Some would say that it's a symptom of taking the "Christ" out of Christmas. The more high-ranking angels have been tasked with investigating this question. They wouldn't let me join in. I had to research what happens if you take the "vents" out of Advent Sunday. The number of vents in Advent Sunday seems to make no difference to anyone. I suspect they gave me the task as a joke. Don't tell Jim, if you see him again. I think he's got the idea I'm a very senior angel. Anyway, can you identify these other angelic campaigns from their descriptions?'

1. Keeping a descriptive name or fixed period in a holiday commemorating the day after Jesus emerged from the tomb.

2. Keeping a word meaning 'proposed or suggested' in a holiday devised for the purposes of a children's game in which 'yes' means 'no' and 'no' means 'yes'.

3. Keeping donations to the poor in a holiday commemorating Jesus's entry into Jerusalem.

4. Keeping air in motion in an annual commemoration of the birth of an English naturalist on 12 February 1809.

5. Keeping a word meaning 'excavation' or 'enjoy' in an annual Shrove Tuesday carnival.

6. Keeping a British word for the buttocks in a holiday which coincides with St Sylvester's Day.

7. Keeping an Egyptian symbol of life in a weekday on which financial institutions are closed.

8. Keeping a word for 'authorize' in the eve of All Saints' Day.

'Oh! My hat!' exclaims Milbert. 'Miss Quincunx!'

You realize that you have pilfered Milbert's hat. He replaces it on his head, only to discover that you have filled it with contraband, forged passports and libellous remarks which you have published and stapled to the sides of the hat with a stolen stapler.

'I didn't notice I was doing it. Why am I filled with a sudden urge to commit crime?'

'It's understandable under the circumstances, Miss Quincunx. Or, should I say, Herod Lemon.'

'*Herod Lemon*?'

# THE BOY WHO LIVED BY HIMSELF

*Hints on page 209*

*Answers on page 252*

## Introduction

Reverend Snakes would murmur, 'To find the path to salvation, start from scratch.' Each Sunday he intoned these words in his sermon at South Bend Penitentiary. Merv and you, serving twenty years for copyright infringement so grave that the judge vomited four times during your trial, listened first with cynicism, later with awe. On the day of your release, you vowed to go straight in the reverend's honour. Vows don't always last.

Every family in town is away for Christmas. Windows of deserted homes are agleam with valuables, and temptation comes slinking into your minds: you'd never dare infringe copyright again, but. . . is there really any harm in a little breaking and entering? Old Man Macbeth shovels snow from the pavement. Rubbing icicles from his beard, he watches the two of you pass, still in your prison uniforms. 'Don't you go near the Von Millicent house!' he barks, thrusting a grizzled thumb in the direction of the house next door. 'Setting out a-robbing, were you?'

'Oh, no, sir!' you chorus.

'Never set foot in that death-shack!' he snarls, slamming his shovel into the pavement. 'Satan incarnate dwells there, in the form of a lonely, sinister boy. There are rumours about him. . . the kind of stories that could make a stone weep and a statue faint. Even the fabulous Von Millicent fortune couldn't induce me to go near the fiend!'

Perhaps Old Man Macbeth should never have mentioned the Von Millicent fortune, for as soon as you and Merv hear the words, your resolve to be free of crime fragments like a blitzed snowman. Slyly you creep to the back door of the Von Millicent house.

*

You detach the Golden Crowbar, a reward for good behaviour as an inmate, from the chain round your neck. How ironic that you're using it for crime! But you force yourself not to think about this. You picture yourself riding a jewel-encrusted tortoise between the emerald rocks of a luxurious beach, sipping champagne and caviar smoothie from a silver vase shaped like a giant high-heeled shoe. The back door gives way with pleasant ease. You are in a dank, musty kitchen. There is a faint smell of rot. It looks like no-one's lived in this house for decades. Old Man Macbeth must have been talking nonsense – probably heard a cat screeching one day and imagined it was some creepy kid. But then Merv's torch illuminates a piece of paper on the table. On top of the page is scrawled, 'Why I Hate My Family by Genghis Von Millicent'.

My parents forge, from a wasp's wing, ersatz pearls.
My aunt and uncle have got my head in a whorl
And oafish Dexter, their son, is acidic with sarcasm.
I'll teach them (like a samurai) long, amusing lessons, throw them in a chasm.
Cousin Brooke clones tarantulas, Rod stole my toothbrush.
Moreover, Megan draws taboo graffiti of a song thrush.
I told Rebecca, 'I'll kill you with punches and ricin!'
'A titch like you? Ha!' She put flesh-eating mice in
My ears, she put ants in my pants!
I can't believe she reduced the bout to ants!
Even a snake deep in a dank fjord, it
Wouldn't stoop to this, no-one would applaud it.
I only wish they hadn't drowned out with the national anthem
A Trixie Mattel concert we went to in Grantham.

*

'Hey, Herod! The kid's concealed the names of sixteen films from *Rolling Stone*'s "Top 100 Films of the 1990s" in his poem. They may be written forwards or backwards, separated by spaces, punctuation or line breaks (for instance, "**No, it cele**brates. . ." would conceal "*Election*").'

'What? What kind of kid does a thing like that? This has gotta be a joke, Merv.'

'I'm gonna see how many I can spot. I'll give myself *half a point* for each one.'

You try to persuade Merv to get out of the house. It's giving you the shivers. Merv, his eyes fixed on the puzzle, shrugs you off. You become absorbed in the puzzle yourself. You read the poem over and over and wonder what happened to the kid's family.

'Looking for money, boys?' simpers a voice. Smirking from the top of the stairs is a blond, pale-faced boy. 'Come and get it!'

'We don't want your money,' you burble. 'We got the wrong address. . . we were just leaving—'

'He's a kid – he can't stop us!' interrupts Merv.

Merv strides forward.

'Not so fast!' screeches Genghis. There's a power in his voice that stops Merv in his tracks and makes your skin prickle. He leaps up and presses a button on the wall. 'You think I'd make it so easy-peasy? I've booby-trapped the stairs. Some steps will trigger paint cans, swinging down and splatting your brains out. Others will let loose armies of my sister Rebecca's flesh-eating mice. I've fed them only cucumbers and sawdust for weeks so they're extra hungry! The other steps just turn the TV off and on. My favourite movie's on. Check out that kid on the screen. Poor little guy, left all by himself, but think what he accomplished! He practically tore those crooks' souls out of their skins. That guy's a hero – changed my life. Now, I'm going to ask you some questions. Fill in your answers in this handy little grid I've drawn on the wall. Then guess which steps are safe! We're starting to have fun, aren't we, boys!'

These are the questions that the child intones:

1. Which chemical element is named after an area of Thessaly in Greece? It's found in chlorophyll and it was recognized as an element by Joseph Black in 1755.

2. Sometimes I hide in Old Man Macbeth's house and give him a little scare. You'll never guess what he has a collection of! It's defined as 'items considered typical of the period from 1837 to 1901'.

3. What did I fire into the belly of the last sneaky man who tried to snatch my family fortune? It's the alter ego of the Marvel superhero Sam Guthrie and the nickname of the jazz musician Julian Adderley.

4. Which politician, who died in 1998, published four poetry collections and *A Lexicon to Herodotus*? He was an inspiration to Nigel Farage, who described him as 'a man who had achieved so much and sacrificed so much for his principles' and who remarked that '[h]ad we listened to him, we would have much better race relations now than we have got.'

5.  I like to draw little asterisks everywhere. What, which the previous answer possessed, links images marked with an asterisk?*

6.  Which word means 'the daughter of an emperor of Russia'? It's an anagram of the surname of the two brothers guilty of bombing the Boston Marathon.

7.  Which word should fill in the blank spaces in these two quotations? Firstly, from Mahatma Gandhi: 'If a person through fear, compulsion, starvation or for material gain or consideration goes over to another faith, it is a _____ to call it conversion.' Secondly, from Richard Hofstadter: 'Veblen spoke often of the intellectual faculty as "idle curiosity" – but this is a _____ in so far as the curiosity of the playful mind is inordinately restless and active.'

8.  Which word means a composition concealing a hidden message in a particular way, like the one in the introduction that leads you towards my little secret?

9.  Which surname is shared by a Kyrgyz mixed martial artist, a nineteenth-century poet exiled for writing satires of Russia's oppression of Ukraine and a former footballer who joined Chelsea for a club record fee in 2006?

10. What's the first name of President William McKinley's assassin as well as the surname of an author of crime novels featuring Guido Brunetti? It's found within the name of a band whose albums include *Because of the Times*.

**Which two steps will harmlessly turn the TV on and off?** ③①
**Now, what's my secret, boys?** Find an instruction. Do it to my ④②
hero. Don't touch his first *i* or his second *e*. Then you'll know, boys.

··········································································

*   There is one asterisk that you have yet to encounter; flick ahead to find it.

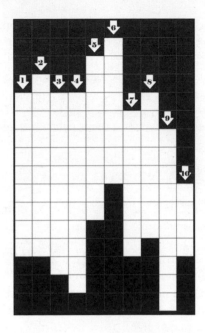

Once more you try to persuade Merv to leave. Once more Merv refuses. He ascends the stairs. You follow cautiously. As Merv's foot touches a step, the TV turns off. With Merv's next step, it bursts into deafening life once more; now the boy on the screen is watching a film where a cackling gangster machine-guns a man to death.

Genghis observes with a serene but mischievous smile. As you reach the top, Merv lunges. Genghis darts away. He opens a door, blows a raspberry, and disappears inside. You and Merv follow. Genghis isn't there. There's nothing but a bricked-up old fireplace with a mantelpiece above it and several objects strewn across the floor. The door behind you slams and you hear a heavy bolt sliding into place.

'Where did he go?' says Merv.

'He's hiding in some secret passage, watching us,' you reply. 'This kid's a pint-size H. H. Holmes. I'm telling you, we should have got out of here.'

'He's just a harmless kid with too much time on his hands. What's he gonna— *aargh!* There's a head there – a human head!'

You approach the head and give its cheek a tentative prod. 'It's a mask. Who is this lady – wasn't she in *Promising Young Woman*? You think the kid made this? What does he do with it?'

Genghis's voice echoes through the room. There must be a speaker hidden somewhere.

'You fall into my traps so easily!' he crows. 'It's like I was the adult and you were the babies. Let me sing you a lullaby, *babies*. . .

> Rock-a-bye burglars, in the spare room,
> When the walls close, you'll both meet your doom. . .'

The walls begin closing in with a sickening crunch, gradually looming closer. If you don't find some way to escape, there'll be nothing left of you but a thin layer of burglar pâté!

'Still think I'm harmless, Mr Burglar Man? Well, I'm gonna give you one chance to save your filthy criminal skins. Each object on the floor represents a single word or name. Look at this enchanting picture of the Von Millicents together. That little antique goes on the far left of the mantelpiece. The three cards go on the far right. You've gotta set out all the objects on that mantelpiece so they form seven consecutive groups of three, going from left to right. Six of those objects overlap between two groups. Now I'm gonna ask you seven questions. The answers will give you clues to what each group has in common.'

1. Which word, which has been mispronounced by presidents Eisenhower, Ford, Carter and George W. Bush, as well as by Homer Simpson from *The Simpsons*, becomes a word meaning 'difficult to see' if its first two letters are swapped round?

2. 'Get ready for rush hour' is the tagline of which 1994 film?

3. Meanings of which word include 'long reverberating sound', 'move on wheels', 'list of names' and 'turn'?

4. The name of which boy band can also mean 'lewd', 'sad' or 'conservative'?

5. What's the most populous state capital in the USA, as well as the first name of Hugh Grant's character in *Paddington 2*?

6. The title characters of the films *Forgetting Sarah Marshall* and *Billy Elliot* are played by actors who share which surname?

7. What is the last word spoken by the title character of Shakespeare's *Hamlet* before he cries, 'O, O, O, O' and dies? It's found in the name of a Simon & Garfunkel song containing the lyrics 'In restless dreams I walked alone / Narrow streets of cobblestone'.

With trembling hands, you and Merv (or the Lunatic Infringers, as you were known) arrange the objects onto the mantelpiece. **In what order do you arrange them?** ㊷

A muffled explosion shatters the bricks blocking the fireplace, peppering debris into your legs. The walls are as close as the sides of a coffin as you and Merv bundle through the gap into the room beyond.

There is no sign of Genghis. This room is bare but for a telephone and a computer on the floor, and a newspaper cutting and a restaurant menu pinned to the wall. The window is open a crack, through which a biting wind howls. The window will open no further.

The newspaper clipping reads:

---

# SHOVEL SLAYER STRIKES AGAIN

With Agnes Reed's body having been discovered last night, police warned that she wouldn't be the last of the South Bend Shovel Slayer's victims. Bystanders heard the screech, "I'll be your pulverizer!" echo ominously through the alley and, rushing towards the murder scene, witnessed the culprit – young, thin, male – inelegantly running away.

---

The menu reads:

# The Compact Caligula

Just dial four digits – 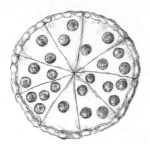 – for your delicious pizza!

### Pepperoni
It's only the finest pepperoni that we use.

### Vegetarian
Peppers, olives, tomatoes and sweetcorn combine to make a pizza as vibrant as the first day of spring!

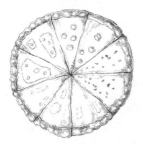

### Four Cheeses
The pizza boasts a winning combination of mozzarella, Stilton, feta and Leerdammer (a Dutch cheese produced by Groupe Bel).

**Margherita**

Tomato and mozzarella – could anything be more
Italian? You forgot to mention the basil – tut tut!

**Frutti di Mare**

Calamari, anchovies, mussels and prawns?
Goodness me!

**Four Seasons**

Ham, artichokes, olives and mushrooms? When
you've tried this, you might want to (in the words
of this pizza's namesake band) 'walk like a man,
my son'!

**Hawaiian**

Ham and pineapple – what a combo! If you're not
tempted, you're not human!

The computer displays this message:

## PASSWORD:

_ _ _ _ _ _ _ _ _

## (type in a 9-letter word)

Once more, Genghis's disembodied voice fills the room from a hidden speaker. 'You must be hungry after all that exercise, boys. Why not order yourselves a pizza? Or you could starve to death. But I don't like it when burglars starve to death. Leaves so much less for the mice to eat.'

'The phone number's crossed out,' you object.

'You'll work it out. Remember the grid I made you fill in? Feels like years ago, doesn't it? A more innocent time. Four words hidden in that grid, across and down, can also be found in the newspaper cutting. The letters either side of those four words in the newspaper cutting spell out four digits.'

**What number do you dial?**  (21)

'You've reached the Pizza Underground,' responds a trembling voice. 'The restaurant where your crust might combust.'

'What do you mean, Pizza Underground?' you demand.

'The menu says, "The Compact Caligula",' adds Merv.

'That was before the kid took it over, sir. He came in every day. We felt sorry for him, this lonely little boy. We let him hang around. We never saw what he was hiding in our restaurant. One day he comes in and says, "You guys work for me now." We all laughed. Hugh – that's the manager – said, "Now I'm the boss round here, young man!" Next thing, the kid's pressed a button, a blowtorch drops from the ceiling and sets Hugh's hair on fire. Everyone's screaming, running for the exit, but the door handle sends ten thousand volts through 'em! And the kid's just watching and chuckling. I still hear that chuckle when I lie awake at night. He's rigged up my whole house with recordings of him chuckling – I've torn the whole place apart trying to find the speakers. . . I haven't slept in weeks. . .

'Now we have to make all the pizzas so they burst into flames when you take a bite. All but one. That's the kid's orders. You gotta work out which pizza's the safe one. He left a message to pass on to you: he's drawn daggers next to objects in the spare room. Each of those objects could be replaced by a different word so that its group still has the same connection. Then you'll know what to order. . .'

**Which pizza do you order?**

After a tense wait, a ladder is propped against the window. A delivery man slides the pizza box through the crack. A boom is heard from beneath, and the ladder – with the shrieking delivery man still clinging on – topples out of view.

You open the box.

Merv is poised to grab a slice.

'Wait a minute, wait a minute!' you say.

'Come on, Herod, I'm starving here.'

'What if the pizza's another puzzle, Merv? Look, we've got a nine-letter password to find. Nine letters, nine slices, you think that's coincidence? Look at the ingredients. . .'

**You type a password. What do you type?**

The computer lights up and spins around, faster and faster, becoming a dizzying blur. The circle of floor on which the computer rests spins with it, and as it spins it sinks like a giant screw. It falls into the room beneath, with a sickening smash and flying sparks.

'You see, Merv?'

'Great. Now there's a hole in the floor. Can I have my pizza now – pretty please?'

'Oh, Mr Burglar Man,' giggles Genghis's voice through the speaker, 'your greed's gonna get the better of you.'

Spikes burst through the ceiling, which begins to descend. . .

You and Merv hurl yourselves through the hole just before the spiked ceiling crunches into the floor.

You land on a filthy dining table which breaks in half. You writhe in pain among splinters of table and shards of computer. The murky, cobwebbed room heaves with rancid, maggot-ridden food.

You hear Genghis's voice. Not so echoey now, more muffled.

'Wicked, mischievous boys – what did you do to my table? I think you're looking for a one-word answer. It can also mean "joke", "attempt" or "sharp sound".'

'What is this, another quiz round?' says Merv.

'Of course,' replies Genghis. 'That was the first question. This round could save your skins, if you follow its advice.'

The questions continue:

2. Ever since you came into this house, you've been trapped in my little cage, with no notion of what awaits you. That reminds me. . . what's that movie where Nicolas Cage sees the future? It's got the same name as a band who released the single 'Too Close', a Michael Crichton thriller and a British chain of clothes shops.

3. Which word can be followed by 'table', 'trip', 'number' or 'robin' to make four phrases?

4. What's the first preposition found in the lyrics to 'The Star-Spangled Banner'?

5. Which word, meaning 'performing' or 'temporarily assuming someone else's duties', follows *This is* to complete the title of a Sia album featuring the songs 'Alive' and 'Cheap Thrills'?

6. On *Room 101*, Meera Syal identified the over-use of which word as a pet hate? 'It's become this all-purpose filler word which means nothing,' she complained. 'It's robbing us of all our descriptive uses of this beautiful language, which it is, and it makes people sound really thick.'

7. 'Scratchy, neopsychedelic guitar riffs nicely contrast the track's hip-hop groove,' commented *Billboard* magazine about which song by EMF, whose title is found within the name of a Radio 4 panel show presented by David Mitchell?

8. One of two characters shares her surname, and the other shares her first name, with different British medallists at the 2008 Beijing Olympics. The surname of the first character and part of the surname of the second can be found in the names (or alter egos) of title characters of Marvel films,

both of whom appear in *Avengers: Endgame*. The first of these characters says of the second, 'She's still mistress here, even if she is dead' – in which work?

'You were looking so sweetly puzzled,' coos Genghis. A portion of the wall slides open and he strides out, a ghoulish smile playing on his lips. You and Merv cower. He pulls a lever disguised as a rancid banana and the floor beneath you and Merv caves in.

You land agonizingly on the concrete floor of a vast, deep basement. It's filled with weapons and human remains. The smell is dizzyingly atrocious.

Genghis peers down. Merv is scratching himself nervously.

'You're nearly out now, boys. All but one exit will lead to your imminent demise. But one exit guides you to the bracing Chicago breeze. And, who knows, you may even make off with the Von Millicent fortune too.'

1. Which stage surname is shared by a saxophonist who released the composition 'Songbird', a rapper whose songs include 'Regulate' (featuring Nate Dogg) and a singer whose songs include 'Ooh. . . Aah, Just a Little Bit'?

2. Peter Boyle and Nicolas Cage play the title characters of two different films sharing which title? It's found within the name of a type of sandwich filled with ground meat and an action figure with the slogan 'America's movable fighting man'.

3. Which two-letter abbreviation may be used to mean 'the temperature at which a given solid will turn to liquid', 'moderately softly' and 'elected representative'?

4. 'Golf', 'rock', 'grub' and 'crawl' can all follow which word to make four phrases?

5. Which three-letter acronym can mean either that a patient mustn't consume food or fluids, derived from a Latin phrase meaning 'nothing through the mouth', or an organization which generates money for a service or a social or political purpose rather than to enrich owners or investors?

6. An actor who plays Emily in *Pitch Perfect 2* and *3*, a singer whose debut solo single was called 'Sign of the Times' and the subject of an ITV drama subtitled *Doctor Death* share which initials?

7. Which word is shared in the name of a band which released the song 'West End Girls', a TV series initially featuring British builders seeking work in Germany and a Stephen King novel containing the line 'Sometimes, Louis, dead is better'?

8. Which initials are shared by a politician and general who wrote the memoir *My American Journey*, a saxophone player nicknamed Bird and an actor who played Andy Dwyer in *Parks and Recreation* and Star-Lord in various Marvel films?

9. Which three-letter word should fill the blank space in each of these Shakespeare quotations? Firstly, from *Romeo and Juliet*, 'How ____ when men are at the point of death /

Have they been merry!'; secondly, from *Julius Caesar*, 'The evil that men do lives after them; the good is ____ interred with their bones'; and thirdly, from *The Merchant of Venice*, 'Signior Antonio, many a time and ____ in the Rialto you have rated me about my moneys and my usances'.

'What do we do now, Herod?' jibbers Merv. 'I can't take it anymore!'

'Think about the Reverend.'

'The Reverend? What's the Reverend gotta do with anything?'

You whisper in Merv's ear. The light of realization flickers in Merv's eyes, then dies down.

'Just follow my lead, OK, Merv?'

**In which grid reference do you find the Von Millicent fortune?** ㊷

**In which grid reference do you find the only safe exit?** ㉛

Soon enough, your arms bulging with jewels, you creep through a cavernous tunnel. Far behind you, Genghis switches on the TV again, and you hear the gravel-voiced gangster intone, 'Keep the change, you filthy animal'. You emerge into a bush behind the house.

You hear the moan of sirens approaching.

'We'll tell them about the kid,' you say.

'They might show us mercy,' says Merv.

A police car draws up. The badge on the car reads: 'THE POLIZZA UNDERGROUND. TO PROTECT AND SERVE GENGHIS.'

'*Run*,' you whisper.

# WINTERLUDE 10

*Answers on page 256*

'To be honest, Milbert,' you gasp as the lights of the police car swell and fill the sky, 'I didn't think I'd get out of there alive.'

'It is rather remarkable, Miss Quincunx,' muses Milbert. For a moment he seems to be impressed. You feel a surge of warmth, but instantly resent the idea that you should care what he thinks of you, when he's just using you to get to Jim and can't even be bothered to disguise it. 'Now tell me,' he continues, 'what do these have in common?'

1. The primary antagonist of the film *Die Hard*; a slogan popularized in the wake of shootings in Paris in January 2015; an illustrated poetry collection subtitled *Shewing the Two Contrary States of the Human Soul*; and an England defender who tweeted in response to Priti Patel following the final of Euro 2020, 'You don't get to stoke the fire at the beginning of the tournament by labelling our anti-racism message as "Gesture Politics" & then pretend to be disgusted when the very thing we're campaigning against, happens.'

2. New Year's; Dirty; Another; and Beautiful.

3. A forename shared by women who married George H. W. Bush, Ringo Starr and the *Family Guy* character Carter Pewterschmidt; Brooklyn, Romeo and Harper's brother; the name that fills the blank space in the *Friends* episode titles 'The One With _____'s Thunder', 'The One With _____'s Boots' and 'The One With Fake _____'; and the forename of a performer who starred with Daniel Craig in both *Knives Out* and *No Time to Die*. (Be specific.)

4. Being hit with a heated iron, shot with a BB gun, covered in feathers, burned after grabbing a heated doorknob and knocked unconscious with a snow shovel.

5. Partridge cartridge, scrounge lounge, porpoise corpus and crackpot jackpot.

6. The author of the classic Christmas story 'The Gift of the Magi', a villain played by Raúl Juliá in the film *Street Fighter*, the frontman of the band Dinosaur Jr., and the author of *The Railway Children*.

7. Anne Boleyn, Harry Bailey, Ira Gershwin and Peppa Pig.

8. The films *Home Alone 2*, *The Little Rascals*, *The Associate*, *Zoolander* and *Two Weeks Notice*.

You reach to scratch your head in thought and discover that you are wearing a crown.

# GOOD QUEEN WESSELSBRON

*Hints on page 210*

*Answers on page 257*

You are Good Queen Wesselsbron, looking out on the Feast of Stephen. The relentless sun beats down. Stretching before you is a tiled floor, all that remains of a once grand castle. The waves lap menacingly at its crumbling edges. Your other castles are located in capital cities. They are lost beneath the water. A disembodied voice rings out through the desolation. 'You have been chosen, Good Queen Wesselsbron. The waters will return to the poles and form ice caps once more. The drowned cities will emerge.'

'Who are you?'

'A strange beast. An unexpectedly coloured animal. I am lonely; you must play a game with me. Only then will you get your precious ice caps back.'

'Where do I find you? What game do you wish to play? What kind of coloured animal are you?'

'You have asked me three questions. I will respond with twenty-six questions of my own. Write your answers upon the tiled floor, so that each horizontal row of tiles contains two answers.'

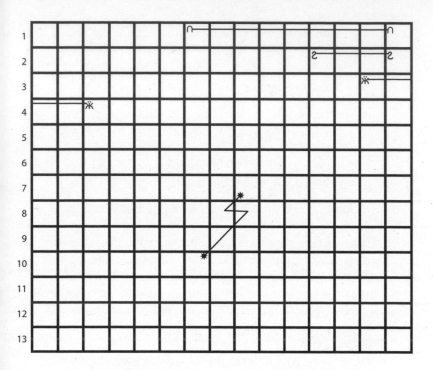

1A. Which object, seen on the flag of a former nation, is found in the name of a group of inherited conditions affecting the red blood cells?

1B. 'Softly', 'spicy', 'fiery', 'attractive' and 'languidly' are examples of adjectives and adverbs; however, '[i]n _____ events, nouns and verbs can be much more helpful than adjectives and adverbs', according to *Modern Trial Advocacy: Analysis and Practice*. Which word (which contains within it a word meaning 'ancient inhabitant of Scotland') should fill the blank space?

2A. Which word, which may denote a type of watercraft, precedes *Soups* in the title of a book of recipes using a hand blender, self-published through Blurb Books? This question may seem impenetrable, but the answer is an anagram of three words within it; four words separate both the first and second and the second and third of these words.

2B. 'Everyone who has ever had a cat can picture exactly, exactly how this scene played, including the part where cat sat in doorway for ages' (*sic*) reads a comment beneath an Imgur post which shows a single pawprint outside a doorway, and which is headed 'How my cat feels about' what? The word I'm looking for is the English-language title of an Orhan Pamuk novel and the stage name of a musician who released the single 'Informer'.

3A. 'Some residents try to slow the shortening of even more hilltops and refuse to sell land; others see the writing on the wall, sell and move away,' is an extract from a *New York Times* review of *The Secret Wisdom of the Earth* by Christopher Scotton, who (according to the *Chicago Tribune*) 'writes with deep understanding about how the mines eventually got played out and the _____ of mountaintop removal'. Which word (also the name of a font often used in Internet memes) fills in the blank?

3B. A 2021 *Guardian* article which accuses the government of 'chipping away at our most valued national institution' claims in its headline that this institution 'is being privatised _____ _____ under the cover of a pandemic'. Which two words fill the blank spaces? The second of these words is one of the few that rhymes with the second word of the name of the institution referred to.

4A. Which song, whose title consists of two rhyming words, gave Jackie Wilson his only UK number one hit?

4B. Meanings of which word include 'moved gradually', 'having a sharpened blade', 'struck (a cricket ball) so that it clipped the side of the bat' and 'furnished with a border'?

5A. Kellogg's, which produces very common cereal brands including Rice Krispies and Crunchy Nut, set up a 'Breakfast Council' of supposedly independent experts, which according to the health news website Stat 'deftly _____ the _____ between cereal promotion and impartial nutrition guidance'. Which two words, which together make up the name of a controversial hit single, fill the blanks?

**5B.** The *Oxford English Dictionary* lists the following among the meanings of which word? 'Designating or representing British territory on a map, usually (now *historical*) with reference to British colonial possessions'; 'Involving or characterized by bloodshed, burning, or violence. Also in extended use'; and '*U.S. Politics*. That votes, or is projected to vote, for the Republican Party, esp. in a presidential election. Also more generally: tending to support the Republican Party; politically conservative.'

**6A.** An organization known by what six-letter name describes itself as 'the only global representative for professional football players'? Together with another organization which shares its first three letters, each year it invites footballers to select players for the men's and women's 'World 11'.

**6B.** Which word denotes molecules which enhance the effect of proteins that act as biological catalysts? The word begins with the surname of filmmaking brothers.

**7A.** According to legend, a river by what name was named in honour of a Celtic princess named Hafren (whose name is Latinized as Sabrina) who was drowned in it by her stepmother? This river is the surname of a mixed martial artist nicknamed 'The Beast'.

**7B.** The locations of Fort Scratchley, New South Wales, and The New Vic Theatre, Staffordshire, share which word in their names with the city where the first Greggs bakery was opened?

**8A.** Which word for a legal practitioner is also used in the USA to mean a canvasser?

**8B.** Which word follows *Bone in the* to complete the title of a crime novel by Anthony Bourdain or 'Cut-Me-Own-' to complete the nickname of a *Discworld* character named Dibbler? The singing techniques of *katajjaq* and *khoomei* are often referred to in English by a phrase which includes this word.

**9A.** A biography by Jacqueline de Romilly of the politician Alcibiades (*c.* 450 BC – 404 BC) discusses Thucydides's account of Alcibiades tricking the Spartans; she points out that 'this kind of unfairness on the part of Thucydides and this hostility toward Alcibiades are _____ _____ elsewhere in the work'. Which two words are missing from this extract, which are associated with the year of Alcibiades' death?

9B. A John Lanchester novel has what single-word title, referring both to its London setting and to the fact that it takes place against the backdrop of the financial crisis? This word denotes something that a company may raise by, for instance, undertaking an initial public offering.

10A. In a BBC drama subtitled *Rather You Than Me*, David Walliams portrayed another comedian, who, like Walliams, changed a single vowel of his surname to make his stage surname. What was this stage surname?

10B. A picture of Sir James Babington, who served as Commander of the British Forces in Italy, was used to depict which fictional character? (Please give your response as an abbreviated rank followed by a surname.)

11A. A general who died in 1863 after being shot by friendly fire (and who is not to be confused with a nineteenth-century White House resident who shared his surname) had what nickname, which is also the name of a charity whose basic aims were drawn up in a 1988 meeting at Ian McKellen's house?

11B. In 2016, Screen Realm wrote of Christopher Nolan's film *Dunkirk*, 'We're a bit under a year away from the release of this one, and time can't _____ _____ enough', and Nolan himself was quoted elsewhere describing the film's atmosphere with the words, 'It's a "fog of war" kind of thing'. Which words – hidden backwards within this question – fill in the blank spaces?

12A. Which word (which, apart from the letter *e* attached to the end, is spelt identically to its English equivalent) follows 'Salon du Livre' to complete the French name for an annual bookfair in Montreal, which in 2020 included a talk entitled 'Antifascism during Pandemic'? It is an anagram of a word found between 'St' and 'College' in the name of a Cambridge college which is spelt identically to an Oxford college except that the Cambridge college uses an *a* where the Oxford college has an *e*.

12B. Which word may precede 'point', 'story', 'letter', 'version' and 'drive' to make phrases?

13A. Which word is included in the title of an album by A Tribe Called Quest featuring 'Jazz (We've Got)', the third instalment of the *Pirates of the Caribbean* film series and the name of an English football team who were the first football league champions?

13B. A *Wired* magazine article headlined 'Why a James Bond film will never premiere on Netflix' has the subheading 'The economics of _____ like *No Time to Die* simply don't work without cinemas. And the pandemic proved it'. Which word fills in the blank – which is also the name of a UK quiz show (based on an American show of the same name) whose first presenter had also voiced James Bond in a 1950s South African radio adaptation of *Moonraker*?

'Now,' continues the voice. 'Think of Ж ✳ used when ∩ Ɛ.' (You cannot comprehend how the voice has expressed these symbols, but it is as if it has etched them onto your brain.) 'One of them may precede five of your answers to make the titles of films. From what is written directly above each of these answers, you will know **where to meet me**. Another may (in some cases loosely) apply to ⑤③ five things hidden diagonally in the grid. These five diagonal things will create two "pockets" of letters which are bordered on all sides by these diagonal things. The letters in the pockets will spell out **the game I want to play.** Exactly seven of your twenty-six answers ④② have the same number of letters. The final one of the Ж ✳ must be applied to these seven answers to produce seven new words or acronyms. Within the twenty-six questions, find seven trios of words which form definitions of these seven new words or acronyms. Take the middle word of each trio, in the order that you find them in the questions – then you will know **what creature I am**.' ⑥③

# WINTERLUDE 11

*Answers on page 259*

'The glorious end of our quest is not far away,' declares Milbert, rising from the sea. 'I didn't think we'd get so far. I'm going to get you out of there, Jim!' he hollers into the void. He turns back to you and asks:

1.  What kind of creature is 'on the Hearth' in the title of a Christmas story by Charles Dickens? The title character of a classic children's book kills one such creature, only for it to return as a ghost, though in a 1940 film adaptation, this creature is given a name which is a minced oath for 'Jesus Christ' and remains alive throughout the film.

2.  Which actor, with the initials SL, portrayed Nick the bartender in *It's a Wonderful Life*? The two most prominent male characters in an American sitcom were named in his honour.

3.  Which song written in the mid-nineteenth century is popularly associated with Christmas, although Christmas is never mentioned in its lyrics? The rarely sung second verse describes the narrator and his companion, Fannie Bright, getting into an accident which is implied to be because of a horse who was 'lean and lank, / Misfortune seemed his lot'.

4.  Thurl Ravenscroft, who performed the song 'You're a Mean One, Mr. Grinch' in the television special *How the Grinch Stole Christmas!*, also spent more than fifty years as the voice of which breakfast cereal mascot?

5.  Unlike most diseases named after people, what do Christmas disease, Hartnup disease and Lou Gehrig's disease have in common?

6. The four-letter first name of a gymnast who won a bronze medal at the 2012 Olympics and went on to win *Dancing on Ice*, the Roman numeral for 500 and a Madeleine L'Engle novel beginning, 'It was a dark and stormy night' combine to form an anagram of the title of which Christmas carol?

7. In Sweden, a compilation of Disney cartoons is traditionally broadcast on Christmas Eve, including one about a bull with what name? A dirigible (which hosts a masquerade ball in Cecil B. DeMille's *Madam Satan*), a car manufacturer with which Jacky Ickx won the 24 Hours of Le Mans four times and a channel separating mainland South America from Tierra del Fuego are named after men who shared this first name (although in the latter case, the man in question is known by this name in English but not in his native language).

8. A Christmas film and a romantic drama film, which were released in the same decade, both inspired namesake Broadway musicals. Both titles are spelt identically to words for the same number in different European languages. Name both films.

Gleaming lights spread out before you.

# DIE, HARDLY

*Hints on page 210*

*Answers on page 260*

Once again, you are in an airport. People jostle past you. Soon it's just you and a man standing before you, holding a sign reading, 'HOLLY MCGLYNN'.

He ushers you into a car. You set off, crawling through the traffic of neon-soaked streets. The windows are down and an intermittent breeze cuts through the warm evening air.

'Lucky it's not Friday,' says the driver. 'That's when the traffic's worst. What kind of place holds a Christmas party in May anyway? How long is it since you saw your husband? Heard he took his old surname back. Silly name if you ask me. You think he invited you to win you back?'

He drops you outside an office building, which stands in a featureless square of grass. 'Mistletoe and Wine' emanates faintly from the upper windows. The music is punctuated by loud bangs.

You open the front door, which leads into the security guard's office. It's dingy, brightened only by a toy with a wild grin which is swaying while juggling coloured balls. Written on its base are the words, 'THIS MACHINE IS SWITCHED OFF AT

WEEKENDS'. There is a stack of books offering guidance on all manner of tasks, entitled: *MILLENNIALS & how to talk to them*; *DUFOURSPITZE, the MATTERHORN & how to climb them*; *WHO'S CONTACTED ME? How to find out*; *DISCO: how to appreciate it*; *KIERKEGAARD & how to understand him*; *A DRAMATIC ENDING & how to build up to it*; *CONFECTIONERY & how to eat it*.

'No terrorists here!' exclaims the security guard. 'And even if there were a terrorist, I wouldn't be able to tell you what their aim was, or what they planned to harness to destroy the world, because they would have microphones everywhere, *if there were a terrorist in the first place*.' She winks furiously. Then she turns tearfully to the portrait of Jodie Comer on her wall. 'I've let you down, Comer! I always wanted to be the best security guard, just like Lani taught me to be, so I could meet you and dazzle you with stories of my prowess!' She turns back to you. 'Lani teaches a course every Tuesday and Wednesday evening on being a good security guard – I've never missed one yet. It's great – lasts the whole evening. I'm Matilda but you can call me Til. Til is the heart of my name – 'cause it's the middle three letters, you see. Let's have a fun quiz. I'll ask you some questions which bear no relation at all to the goals of any terrorists.'

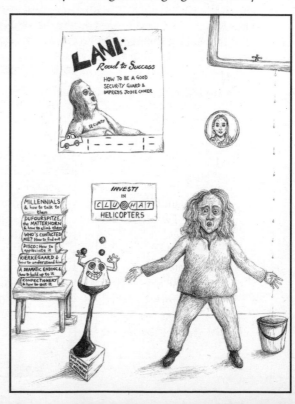

1. Which city is 663 miles east (and slightly north) of our city and hosts an International Balloon Fiesta? The film *High School Musical* is set (though not filmed) there and, in a recurring joke, Bugs Bunny ends up in an unexpected place after failing to take a left turn there.

2. The building in Illinois known as the Edith Farnsworth House is among the most famous buildings of Ludwig Mies van der Rohe, an architect who once said, 'The individual is losing significance; his _____ is no longer what interests us.' Which word fills the blank space? This word also concludes the title of a film starring Tenacious D, a band which was formed in our city.

3. 'The event is set to take place on November 9, a week before the Brazilian Grand Prix and will follow a similar structure to previous events with the inclusion of live music in addition to esports and pitstop challenges,' wrote *Motorsport* magazine in January 2020 on a planned fan festival to honour the life of which man, who was the subject of a documentary film by Asif Kapadia?

4. Occurring on what the *New York Times* describes as a father and son's 'cruise around their small town seeking the culprits' who have stolen the father's tools, which Bob Nelson film has a two-word title (a three-letter word followed by a twelve-letter word) which refers to the fact that the boy is supposed to be preparing to undergo a Christian rite of passage?

5. Day of the Dead was established as a celebration in our city partly thanks to the efforts of the Mexican-American artist Beto de la Rocha, whose son Zack is the frontman of which band? Zack explained that he chose the band name because 'I wanted to think of something metaphorically that would describe my frustrations toward America, toward this capitalist system and how it has enslaved and exploited and created a very unjust situation for a lot of people.'

6. 'Month of May / The Suburbs' by Arcade Fire and 'The Money Store' by Death Grips are among the many tracks and albums reviewed by YouTuber Anthony Fantano on his channel The Needle Drop. Fantano also contributed to

what *Wired* magazine in 2018 described as 'the weirdest film you'll see this year': a fan-made retelling of which 2001 film, which was itself based on a book which concludes, 'And they lived horribly ever after, scaring the socks off all who fell afoul of them'?

7. Comer means to carry on starring in masterpiece after masterpiece, but my favourite show she's been in is *Killing Eve*. *Den of Geek* wrote that 'every once in a while, Eve and Villanelle meet and, more times than not, it means' what? The word I'm looking for concludes the title of a suite by Händel which was written for an outdoor celebration of the end of the War of the Austrian Succession.

8. What in Spanish is known as an *espadachín*? The English equivalent I'm looking for, denoting a male fighter, is an anagram of a word meaning 'creatures found in Frank Herbert's *Dune* novels whose larvae produce a drug called melange'.

'Get to the heart of every answer,' says Til, and winks very furiously indeed. 'Now, let me introduce you to the staff having an unremarkable Christmas party. It's not like one of them is secretly the terrorist and there's a hidden indication of which one it is!' She presses her face close to yours so you don't overlook her winking.

She leads you into a room containing a huge computer called the 'Obe Babe'. A calendar on the wall has the following entries: *May 7th, 10am: Juggle-o-Matic to be installed*; *May 13th, 9am: Leaky pipe in guardroom to be fixed*; *May 17th: IT support to fix 'BABE' (display shows L where R is meant + vice versa)*. Seven anxious employees are assembled, who eye you without recognition. 'I'll introduce you to some of the staff. Going from left to right: this is Gerald Smitz, a high-ranking military officer; Wilmington Flit, the accountant; Psi Veldt, who holds inquests into deaths at the office; Stacey Marmamite, the puppeteer hired to provide the entertainment; Heath Veldt, Psi's husband; Adeola Obe, the head of the Obe Corporation; and Henry Susufruss, who looks after the iguanas in the basement. Anthony Von Saint Tibbins-Ibbs, the events organizer, hasn't been seen all day. Why don't we have another quiz, everyone?'

1. Silent follows Greatest, which follows Lost. Which ten-letter word follows all three?

2. Which word is found in the English-language names of an item manufactured by Victorinox, a reinsurance company which commissioned 30 St Mary Axe ('the Gherkin') and a Johann Wyss novel about a couple and their sons who become castaways on an island in the East Indies?

3. Which word follows 'Shot' to complete the title of a French Montana single or precedes 'Herrin' in the title of a Scots

folk song (as it can be a Scottish word for 'fresh')? It also follows 'The Daily' to make the name of a right-wing American news and opinion website.

4. Which word was a British nickname for a French leader, as well as the title of an Australian detective series whose title character is the French leader's namesake and shares this nickname? In the books which inspired the TV series, this nickname is spelt without the letter *e*.

5. Which word, which is found within the surname of the director of the 1967 film *The Jungle Book*, precedes 'Way' in the title of a Chris Stapleton song?

6. Which word is shared in the names of the USA's longest-running radio show, an event whose winners include Nicolaus Silver and Gay Trip, and a 1997 video game whose European cover art depicts Trump Tower?

7. Which word, whose meanings include 'clothes', is also a short first name shared by a frontiersman after whom a US state capital is named and an actor who portrayed his ancestor Robert Catesby in the BBC series *Gunpowder*?

'Think about my guardroom – and think backwards!' hisses Til, winking more and more.

**What does the terrorist plan to harness, in order to unleash it and destroy the world? (This plan strikes you as confused from a scientific point of view.) A two-word answer is required.**

**What is the hidden message of Round 2, which will help you work out the terrorist's identity?** 🄜🄟

**Who is the terrorist?** 🄜🄟

'Why don't I show you our top-secret safe?' suggests Til.

'Not so fast!' yells the terrorist, producing a gun. 'You've cottoned on, haven't you? I knew I shouldn't have pinned my escape plan to the wall. Stay there.' You and Til join the remaining hostages.

'Why don't we cheer ourselves up with a quiz?' suggests Til.

1. Which word for a religion becomes the surname of the composer of *24 Caprices for Solo Violin* if its final two letters are replaced by two different letters?

2. A Suzanne Collins novel set in the *Hunger Games* universe is titled *The Ballad of* what *and Snakes*? The nine-letter word I'm looking for contains only two vowels.

3. 'It's Uncle Bimbo!' is an anagram of which word?

4. Which word, meaning 'cover', is an anagram of both the name of a philosopher ordered to commit suicide after being suspected of involvement in a conspiracy to murder Nero and a word meaning a spiritualist meeting?

5. Three chemical elements are spelt differently in British and US English: sulphur, aluminium and which other?

6. The name of which bird of the genus *Delichon* can be formed from the first name of an actor preceded by the final word of the title of a film in which he starred as an FBI agent who must go undercover as a grandmother?

7. 'We admitted we were powerless over alcohol – that our lives had become unmanageable' is a notable first what? The word I'm looking for also fills the blank space in Justin Bieber's first autobiography *First _____ 2 Forever*.

'We need a distraction,' Til whispers. 'Think of a synonym for the first answer, white-rumped examples of the second whose name evokes parts of a cereal grain, a synonym for the third answer, a synonym for the fourth, the symbol for the fifth, the surname of a musician who may be described as the sixth answer and the stage name of a musician who may (in the same way) be described as the seventh. Five of the seven words you end up with contain the second word of the very thing the terrorist wishes to harness. Where this word appears, remove it to make a new word; where it is absent, add it to make a new word. You see, I know all the gossip around here, and I know which item you need to draw attention to if you want to cause a distraction.'

**What is the hidden message of this round, which instigates an uproar among the hostages?** ㊷

The hostages clamour. As some of them try to wrest the gun from the terrorist's grasp, Til guides you to a little room containing a safe. 'In here,' she explains, 'is the key to our CLU-HAT helicopter. The terrorist intends to escape to freedom. Here's a quiz round so you can work out the combination.'

'You can just tell me – the terrorist's too distracted to hear us now.'

'I do love quizzes, though.'

1.  Which word comes next in this extract from a Christina Rossetti poem? 'It's surely summer, for there's a swallow: / Come one swallow, his mate will follow, / The bird race quicken and wheel and. . .' Plots are often known to perform this action.

2.  'Eye', 'lay' and 'bear' may all precede which word? The word 'testicle' derives from the Latin for this word, presumably as testicles were thought to provide evidence of their bearer's virility.

3.  Which word completes this Jimmy Carr joke: 'I got talking to a North African girl in her native language for hours. We just. . .'? (The joke would have been more accurate if Carr had said 'Southern African'.) Meanings of this word include 'suddenly became clear'.

4.  A Scorpions album, a comedy horror film and a reality TV franchise all have titles which play on the same phrase. The album replaces the last word with 'Sting'; the film replaces the last word with 'Bite'; and the franchise replaces the first word with 'Married'. What are the middle two words?

5.  Which word meaning 'letter' can be preceded by three different sets of three letters to mean, respectively, 'tolerant', 'refusing to treat something or someone as worthy of consideration', and 'inclined to yield to others' authority'?

6.  Mark 'Bez' Berry was known for playing which instrument in the Happy Mondays? I'm looking for a plural answer which is an anagram of a cosmetic.

She hands you a card which reads:

*Foolish; bird; capital city; lead a bad life*
*Dense vegetation made a bird-like sound*
*Enormous propelled weapon*
*Hackneyed bird*
*Spoil a feline; eager*
*Foolish*

*When semi-colons appear, each position is joined to the next, moving from left to right – otherwise, when two positions appear, they are overlaid.*

## What is the four-digit combination?

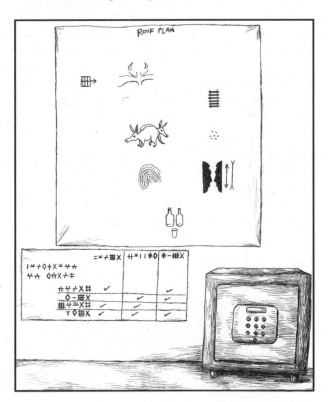

You retrieve the helicopter key.

'Lastly,' says Til, 'you must make it to the helicopter before the terrorist finds you and snatches the key from your grasp. There are various items on the roof that must be traversed in the correct order; if you do so, the helicopter is summoned. On the left of the roof plan is where you emerge from the stairwell. The names of the items on the roof are significant; from them you will deduce an important message.'

1. Which sinister-sounding three-word name is shared by a hiking route in the Catskills and a Japanese crime film? It is an anagram of the first names of a husband and wife and their shared surname.

2. Cyril Sneer, a character in the Canadian animated series *The Raccoons*, and Cerebus, the title character of comics by Dave Sim, are fictional examples of what animals? The fictional character Arthur Read is one of these animals, and in his first appearance, in the book *Arthur's Nose*, is depicted as being embarrassed about his long nose, which is shown as much shorter in later incarnations.

3. Which word fills the blank space in this quotation from Simon & Garfunkel's 'The Sound of Silence': 'Because a vision softly creeping / Left its _____ while I was sleeping'? This word concludes the name of a band whose past members have included Mick Harvey and Blixa Bargeld.

4. Which word completes this film title: *Pokémon: Zoroark: Master of* _____? If the first letter of this word is replaced by *a*, it becomes a word meaning 'implicit references'.

5. Which two-word term for a fingerprint pattern, if its first two letters are swapped round and the second word is spelt backwards, becomes the title of a 1985 video game in which players pot balls against a backdrop resembling the surface of the Moon?

6. Which word fills the blank space in this quotation from William Shakespeare – 'A substitute shines brightly as a king / Until a king be by, and then his state / _____ itself, as doth an inland brook / Into the main of waters' as well as this quotation from William Hague – 'You worked so

hard you didn't feel you'd drunk 10 pints by four o'clock, you used to sweat so much. But then you had to lift all the \_\_\_\_\_ off the lorry. It's probably horrifying but we used to do that then go home for tea and then go out in the evening to the pub'?

7. Which word, which follows 'Ruby on' to make the name of a web-application framework, has meanings including 'birds', 'bars' and 'complains fiercely'?

**What is the hidden message?**

You ascend the stairs to the roof and trace your path carefully. The helicopter descends towards you. You unlock the door. The occupant of the helicopter greets you with a roguish smile.

# WINTERLUDE 12

*Answers on page 264*

Centre stage stands the helicopter. It dissolves as you approach it. The sky fades into blackness apart from a single cloud, which extends fluffy tentacles. The tentacles writhe into the shape of Milbert. 'Miss Quincunx, we are close,' effuses Milbert. 'Tell me, do you have a New Year's resolution?' Without waiting for a response, he continues, 'Mine is to be a vegan. As Jim's guardian angel, I would read *Vegan Life* magazine when I followed him to the dentist. I always did have a fondness for honey, though – I shall miss stirring it into my tea. Let's get into practice with this quiz round. Each question has two answers. The two answers are spelt identically except that the first answer must have a "non-vegan" string of letters removed to make the second answer (spaces may also be added and removed). For example, a pair of answers could be "screaming: sing". Have one point for each pair.'

1. Doused with alcohol and set alight: supply.

2. Made known: a slender-leaved plant or its stalk.

3. Having a varus deformity: dismissed in a particular way.

4. A radio drama first broadcast in 1954: the surname shared by Tony and Rory, the first brothers to play rugby union for England together since 1937.

5. The two words which fill the blank space in this definition from Jean Gallier and Jocelyn Quaintance's *Linear Algebra and Optimization with Applications to Machine Learning* – 'A pair $(R, S)$ such that $A = RS$ with $R$ orthogonal and $S$ symmetric positive semidefinite is called a _____ of $A$': 'Annabel Lee' or 'The Fall of the House of Usher'.

6. Someone who interviews people who have completed an assignment and reports on their answers: postpone.

7. Type of bed: inauthentic.

8. A statement concerning the difference between two numbers: the four words which fill the blank space in this *Manchester Evening News* headline from September 2020 – 'Should you call police if you _____ people in your neighbour's garden?'

'Why are we having a New Year's round?' you demand. 'What happened to all the Christmassy stuff?'

'Christmassiness is crumbling around us,' responds Milbert. 'It is losing its hold, for we're within reach of freedom. Freedom for you, Jim! We have but one quest to go – but it is a fearsome one. You must choose one of four bodies to inhabit.'

# INTO THE FRIDGE

*Hints on page 212*

*Answers on page 265*

Choose which of the four siblings to play as:

**PEDRO**: begin on page **155**.

**SADIE**: begin on page **157**.

**ERICK**: begin on page **160**.

**LAKRISHA**: begin on page **163**.

When you have finished one page, continue to the next unless directed elsewhere. You will want to return to previous pages to solve puzzles which will grow clearer as you go on. In case you get lost, this is the path each character takes from beginning to end:

**PEDRO**: 155-165-185-174-186-178-188

**SADIE**: 157-165-183-174

**ERICK**: 160-165-182-174

**LAKRISHA**: 163-165-171-(mystery page)-174

When keeping track of your points for this round, you may only count the points accumulated by *one* sibling. You may, however, play as multiple siblings in turn and gain the points accumulated by the highest-scoring one.

# PEDRO

When you first encounter the Professor hunched over a desk in the study of his vast, creaky house, he winks and hands you a little card. On it is written:

**I have always dreamed of encountering wolves.**

A tiller of the ground; vengeance shall be taken sevenfold upon whosoever slayeth him

*My dream home is sited near where four stand united. Find my home if you aim for what gives me my name.*

'Is this about me?' you ask. He ignores you, once more absorbed in his studies. All but the first line means little to you. But every morning for years you have woken, shivering, from nightmares in which your toothbrush has turned out to be an unconventionally shaped wolf and bitten you on the tongue. How on earth could the Professor have known?

When Sadie discovered how to open the passageway within the fridge, she summoned you and your siblings. You ventured through the fridge into Mevania, emerging beside a lamppost. When Lakrisha had told you all about her adventures there, you had mocked her – and Erick, who had had his own secret encounter in this snow-cloaked land, had mocked her most cruelly of all. Now you follow in reverential silence as Lakrisha leads you to the home of Mr Ringo, the faun she had befriended. The door to his cottage hangs open. It is barren except for a single poster on the wall (showing a quartet of mice accompanied by the words 'FACE MELT IN BOTTOM') and a map of Mevania which you retrieve from a table.

A note is pinned to the door, signed, 'Ethelbert, Captain of the Silver Sorceress's Secret Police'.

'Look!' cries Sadie. 'There are seven items of furniture hidden in Ethelbert's message! Each may be found forwards or backwards, separated by spaces, line breaks or punctuation! Each has at least five letters, and no letter overlaps between more than one item of furniture! Let's find them, for half a point each!'

'And see here, everyone!' adds Lakrisha. 'Five well-known fictional lions are hidden in the message too! They're formed from alternate letters, the way that "Alex" would be formed from *All-New X-Men*! Each one's got at least six letters and no letter overlaps between more than one! Oh, do let's find them all, for another half-point each!'

**Go to page 165.**

When the Professor first encountered you, he pressed a card into your hand.

    3       4       5

**WHEN I WRITE A NUMBER, I CONVERT IT INTO**
FOUND GRACE IN THE EYES OF THE LORD WHEN THE   **ROMAN NUMERALS.**
EARTH WAS CORRUPT; LATER PLANTED A VINEYARD AND   **I HAVE ALWAYS**
CURSED CANAAN AFTER BEING SEEN NAKED BY HAM   **DREAMED**
**NARNIA'S MAKER IS FLED. WITH A TANGO INSTEAD, IF I SHUFFLE THE SPELLING,**   **OF MEETING**
                **I'LL FIND MY**   **A BEAVER.**
    1       2       **DREAM**
                       **DWELLING.**

How curious! It is quite true that you have always fantasized about encountering beavers, whose company, you imagine, is far superior to that of humans – and, whenever you are asked a question where the answer is a number, you really do write a Roman numeral instead! But the note about 'Narnia's maker' is very baffling. You ponder what it could mean. Perhaps the word 'is' must be removed from something? And is there a reference to the NATO Phonetic Alphabet?

'I *had* felt like going on an adventure,' the Professor murmurs to himself. 'But I just can't recall. . . I'm sure the woman I'm supposed to name shares her forename with a character in that book. . . you know, the one about the children who go into a stationery cupboard or something. You!' He looks up, suddenly aware of your presence once again. 'Savannah, was it, or Serenity? Would you rearrange the objects in my fridge? I think, if you do, it's supposed to give a message. . .' It was the very fridge which Lakrisha claimed to have passed through into a magical land – though no-one believed her, of course. As the Professor wanders from the room, you begin to reorder his bizarre collection – a copy of Joanna Newsom's *Ys*, a book with one word missing from its title – *The World ___ And Book of Facts 2020* – a girl hypnotized into semi-consciousness, and so much more. You wonder where on earth the Professor keeps his food. But by the time your siblings come in, you are feverish with excitement. You have discovered the hidden message – revealing how to access the secret world beyond the fridge. **What is the nine-word message?**

⑤③

The four of you pass through the fridge to the magical, snowy land
of Mevania, emerging beside a lamppost. Mr Ringo's cottage, where
Lakrisha has been before, is barren except for a poster on the wall
(showing a quartet of mice accompanied by the words 'FACE MELT
IN BOTTOM') and a map of Mevania which you retrieve from a
table. A note is pinned to the door, signed, 'Ethelbert, Captain of
the Silver Sorceress's Secret Police'.

'Look!' you cry. 'There are seven items of furniture hidden in Ethelbert's message! Each may be found forwards or backwards, separated by spaces, line breaks or punctuation! Each has at least five letters, and no letter overlaps between more than one item of furniture! Let's find them, for half a point each!'

'And see here, everyone!' adds Lakrisha. 'Five well-known fictional lions are hidden in the message too! They're formed from alternate letters, the way that "Alex" would be formed from *All-New X-Men*! Each one's got at least six letters and no letter overlaps between more than one! Oh, do let's find them all, for another half-point each!'

**Go to page 165.**

When the Professor first met you, he handed you a card and advised that it would come in handy on your adventures. What an oddball. The card reads:

I have always wanted to meet a witch.

**A keeper of sheep; the LORD had respect unto his offering of the firstlings of his flock and of the fat thereof**

*The dot that marks my dream abode dwarfs the one across the road.*

When Lakrisha first enters the fridge, you follow, emerging beside a lamppost. But you lose sight of her, instead encountering an imperious woman in a sleigh who is very keen to find out all about you and your brother and sisters. A fork materializes in her hand; dipping it into the depths of the sleigh, she spears a lustrous cube and dangles it into your mouth. It is a cube of tofu. You have never tasted tofu before and had always regarded it with contempt, but it is the most sumptuous thing that has ever crossed your lips.

'Zippity-zoppity-zow!' you exclaim impulsively, immediately ashamed of this bizarrely childish outburst.

1. 'There's a whole tray where that came from,' she croons. 'It's from a traditional dish called Buddha's delight. I couldn't possibly finish it all. If only I had a brave young man to help me.' The more that you look at the tray, its lid adorned with glimmering stars, the more a thought worms its way into your head. **What is it?**

2. 'You and your brother and sisters must join me at my delightful castle. You're a clever boy, you'll work out where to find it. Take this – it looks like an innocent map of the London Underground, so no-one will suspect. Find two words that remind you of the sumptuous delicacy you have just consumed. The first will make you think of a sweeter treat; the second will make you think of the crimson heavens. The quickest route from the first to the second will provide you with directions to my castle. You will know when the time is right to come to me; the last three of one, the first three of the next. . .'

**What are the directions to the castle?**

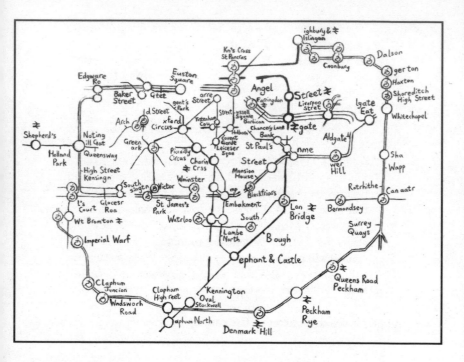

The next time you venture through the fridge, you are accompanied by Pedro, Sadie and Lakrisha. You sense that they resent you for teasing Lakrisha and pretending she was lying about the fridge, and you resent them right back. Mr Ringo's cottage, where Lakrisha has been before, is barren except for a poster on the wall (showing a quartet of mice accompanied by the words 'FACE MELT IN BOTTOM') and a map of Mevania on the table. You pick up the map.

As your siblings natter insipidly about hidden clues in the message, you notice (far more cleverly) that consecutive words found within it spell out anagrams of six well-known witches from fiction, folklore and legend. Each contains at least eight letters and no letter overlaps between more than one witch. You decide to award yourself a point for each one you spot.

**Go to page 165.**

When you first encounter the professor, he is gazing into an open fridge filled with a bizarre assortment of items, none of which appears to need refrigeration. 'Shaparak Khorsandi? No,' he murmurs. You clear your throat and he spins round. 'Oh, hello! You must be one of those children who've come to stay with me. I felt like another adventure, but I'll be blowed if I can remember. . . Sophie Duker? Sue Perkins? No? Oh, never mind.' He places a card in your hand and meanders out of the room. On the card are these words:

#### I have dreamed of meeting Aslan.
'In sorrow thou shalt bring forth children', said the Lord God unto her

> *This is the place that a crow can reach sooner*
> *Flying away from the fruit ship of Spooner*

What a curious card! Yet it is true that you have always dreamed of encountering Aslan, the majestic lion from *The Chronicles of Narnia*. You imagined yourself in the shadow of his gentle but mighty presence, shielded from the world's onslaughts. But the rest of the card's words are a mystery. And how oddly the Professor was behaving! As you absent-mindedly recite the names of other comedians, the back of the fridge creaks open to reveal a wintry world beyond. You pass through, emerging beside a lamppost. A faun, Mr Ringo, invites you to his cottage and plays a melody. 'A terrible sorceress rules this land,' he warns. 'Her most fearsome follower is Ethelbert, an ice-skating wolf! If they find out I've been harbouring you. . .' He looks round nervously. 'If anything does happen to me, seek out my neighbours, the Beavers. My tune and three questions they will ask once you are within their house will bring you reassurance.'

The following week, when Sadie discovered how to open the passageway within the fridge, she summoned you and your siblings. The four of you ventured through the fridge into Mevania, emerging beside a lamppost. When you had told your brothers and sister about your adventures there, they had mocked you – and Erick, who had had his own secret encounter in this snow-cloaked land, had mocked you most cruelly of all. Now they follow in reverential silence as you lead them to the home of Mr Ringo. The door to his cottage hangs open. It is barren except for a single poster on the wall and a map of Mevania which you retrieve from a table.

A note is pinned to the door, signed, 'Ethelbert, Captain of the Silver Sorceress's Secret Police'.

'Look!' cries Sadie. 'There are seven items of furniture hidden in Ethelbert's message! Each may be found forwards or backwards, separated by spaces, line breaks or punctuation! Each has at least five letters, and no letter overlaps between more than one item of furniture! Let's find them, for half a point each!'

'And see here, everyone!' you add. 'Five well-known fictional lions are hidden in the message too! They're formed from alternate letters, the way that "Alex" would be formed from *All-New X-Men*! Each one's got at least six letters and no letter overlaps between more than one! Oh, do let's find them all, for another half-point each!'

**Continue to the next page.**

The note reads:

> *Ringo has been fraternizing with twits (we checked, of course). How indiscreet, testifying to his tendency to speak rashly. Eeyore-like, illumined by a moonbeam, he wasn't laid on normal furniture but was squatting down, avidly listening to a gay ABBA tribute band, Face Melt in Bottom – and this is when out of the corner where I'd hidden to watch and listen I backflipped and arrested him! No-one will escape justice, not even if they are the child of aristo, oligarch, the offspring of mangy earl, noble dynasty's scion! What rude 'loyal' bicorns there are, refusing to disclose the truth to the Silver Sorceress. Such creatures engorge her arm in might, so she could lift any dumbbell! I herd them to be boiled in a saucepan, accused in a lawcourt (lads clump, await lily ice cream, watch and jeer), hanged from the infamous flagstaff, then turned to stone!*

Can you find the hidden things you are looking for?

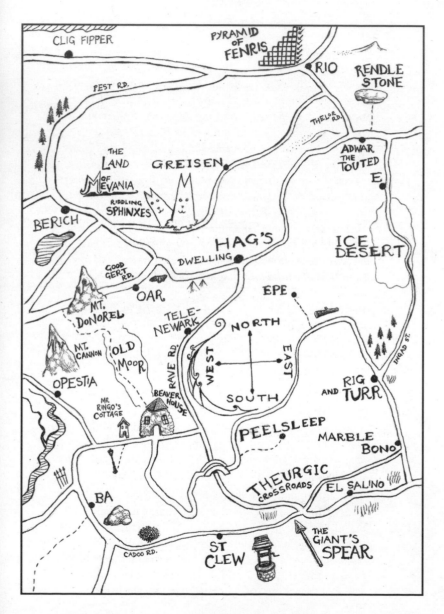

# CHAPTER 1: SUSPICIOUS BEAVERS

'What do we do now?' demands Pedro. 'There's some mighty peculiar stuff going on, with secret police and sorcery and whatnot. It'd be best to head back in that fridge.'

'We can't abandon Mr Ringo to his fate!' Lakrisha expostulates. 'He said if he was ever in trouble, we should go and see his neighbours the Beavers.'

You knock on the Beavers' door.

'Who goes there?' responds a squeaky voice. 'Sorceress's minions, I'll be bound.'

'We're not!' says Erick.

'Can you prove it?' demands the voice within. 'Tell me what my favourite Western is. There's an ancient prophecy that four humans would come to this land, and to prove that they'd come in good faith, they'd be able to tell me what my favourite Western is – after I'd asked them six questions. Here they come.'

1. Which four-letter word is shared in the titles of a single by Coldplay with guest vocals by Beyoncé and a song adapted into a football chant, with 'Tottenham Hotspur', 'to the Hibees' or 'Man United' (for example) replacing one word of its chorus?

2. Meanings of which word include 'fate or destiny', 'item or set of items for sale' and 'large number'?

3. Which word concludes the titles of a Fred Astaire and Ginger Rogers film featuring the song 'Cheek to Cheek' and a book which begins, 'The sun did not shine. It was too wet to play. So we sat in the house all that cold, cold, wet day'?

4. The central character of Louis Sachar's *Holes*; a former Prime Minister of Cambodia (as his name is usually rendered in English) who led a coup to overthrow Prince Norodom Sihanouk; the county town of Meath: find locations in Mevania which share the property that these have in common. How many times does the first letter of your name occur within the names of these locations?

5. If you truly are the ones foretold in the prophecy, you should each have a card. Which character from the Book of Genesis is described in the card?

6. The card contains a rhyme, describing a place where you dream of living – though you may not know it yet. Look at Ringo's map! That place lies in Mevania. What is its name?

7. Mix your answers up with the one whom you dream of encountering. What is our favourite Western?

# CHAPTER 2: THE DISAPPEARANCE OF ERICK

The Beavers let you in.

'There's no time to lose!' squeaks Mrs Beaver. 'We must find Su Samuru.'

'Who?' says Lakrisha, heart pounding. The sound of this strange name sends a shiver of awe through all four children.

'The true ruler of Mevania. He is the only one who can stop the sorceress. But how to avoid her minions? The prophecy says we must ask you seven questions, then you will tell us which direction to go in.'

1.  Which Scottish or German expression of emotion is spelt identically to an abbreviation for a network such as BACS, which coordinates electronic payments and automated money transfers?

2.  Which word, which forms the name of an American retail corporation, can be followed by 'practice', 'market' or 'audience' to make three phrases?

3.  The surnames of Egon, a Budapest-born restaurant critic, Mary, the first female CEO of General Motors, and Damian and Naomie, who starred in *Our Kind of Traitor*, are shared with members of a group known in English by what two-word name (the first word of which has five letters and the second word eight)?

4.  Which word may precede 'frog' or 'line' or may follow 'Greek' or 'dawn' to make four phrases?

5.  Meanings of which word include 'ornamental fabric', 'cord or string' and 'add an ingredient, such as alcohol, to'?

6.  Which word is the name of a fictional sword, the ring name of a wrestler, and the stage name of a musician the title of whose album *Ten Summoner's Tales* makes a pun on his surname?

7.  Which two-word title is shared by a 1970 song which begins, 'I'll light the fire' and a 1982 song which provides the title for a jukebox musical?

'Four is a sacred number,' declares Mr Beaver. 'Sets of four will lead you in the right direction! You see, just as there are four of you, there are four of each— hang on! There are only three of you! What happened to that shifty-looking boy?'

**Erick is sought in vain. He has gone to join the Sorceress. In which direction must Pedro, Sadie, Lakrisha and the Beavers go to find Su Samuru and avoid the Sorceress's minions?** (42)

Pedro: Go to page 185.
Sadie: Go to page 183.
Erick: Go to page 182.
Lakrisha: Continue to the next page.

## What was your message of reassurance from Mr Ringo?

After you have walked for many hours, you hear rustling. At first you recoil in fear, then a wonderstruck excitement overcomes you. You have the unshakeable feeling that you are about to meet Su Samuru. A diminutive otter emerges from a bush.

'Welcome, children,' he intones grandly. 'It is I, the true ruler of Mevania.'

'*You're* Su Samuru? I thought you'd be a lion.'

'A *lion*? Why on earth would I be a lion?'

'Well,' says Sadie, 'there was this note with lions hidden in it.'

'So? I once did a jigsaw that had a picture of a slug. Did I decide that a completely random person was a slug? No, 'cause I'm not a big prat!'

'Your majesty,' cuts in Pedro hastily, 'truly, it is an honour—'

'A *lion* as king of Mevania – I ask you! It would have ripped your faces off as soon as look at you. You wouldn't have time to kneel before it because it would have gobbled up your knees! Very regal behaviour, *I don't think*!'

The otter is breathing heavily now and takes a minute to calm down. Then he announces in a deep, imposing voice, 'The Silver Sorceress has turned your brother to stone. Tomorrow we must save him. Tonight we rest.'

It is growing dark. With an authoritative little paw, he motions you towards a little hollow beside the road.

You awake to the sound of sleigh bells. Is it the Silver Sorceress advancing towards you? No! It's a Christmas elf. He gives magical and dangerous gifts to Pedro and Sadie, and you hold your breath to see what powerful present awaits you. It's a pencil and a sheet of paper.

On the back of the page the following text is written:

*Don't want to engage in battle or <u>minister</u> to the sick? We <u>suspect</u> you'd prefer to spend your <u>time</u> being a <u>mover</u> and shaker in the shading-by-numbers world!*

*This fabulous pencil comes with a free 'Sorceress's Castle' illustration that will provide minutes upon minutes of fun!*

*EXCHANGE POLICY: This product may be exchanged for one other item. Add up the numbers in the parts you have shaded in (using the hidden clue as your guide) to make a page number. On the page you are directed to, take the middle two words of each sentence to form two new sentences (the first of which is six words long) describing the item you have exchanged the pencil and paper for; these sentences direct you to three answers within this quiz. These three answers lead you to a hidden message telling you the name of another object you may exchange the second item for.*

**The shading-by-numbers puzzle, which reveals the item you exchange the pencil and paper for, directs you to which page?** 42 (Once you have examined that page, return here.)

**What is the hidden message revealing the object for which you exchange the second item?** (You will not be able to uncover this hidden message yet – come back to it at the end of the quiz.) 53

The following day Su Samuru takes you to the Sorceress's castle. He extends a paw towards the stone figures of Erick and Mr Ringo; a sound emerges like the tinkling of a harp, and they spring into life – Mr Ringo exuberant and Erick shamefaced. Laid out upon the tiles are more stone creatures.

## CHAPTER 3: AT THE SORCERESS'S CASTLE

'Can you save all of them too, Su Samuru?' asks Lakrisha.

'The Sorceress has turned some of her most loyal servants to stone, to trick those who return them to life,' intones Su Samuru. 'They'd tear off our limbs without so much as a "by your leave". Those who correspond to the answers to these questions are the ones we must save.'

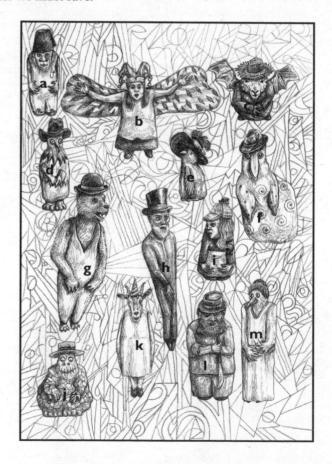

1. Which word, meanings of which include 'the way something is laid out' and 'be situated', is spelt identically to the surname of the first UN Secretary-General?*

2. The names of a long-running American reality TV series whose many spin-offs have included the short-lived *Dash Dolls* and *Flip It Like Disick*, a rock band whose songs include 'Aerials' and 'Chop Suey!', a Robert Wyatt studio album featuring 'Sea Song' and a Susanna Clarke novel about two magicians each contain a what?

3. What does each of the following have in common with the others: a square in Barcelona dominated by a monument to Doctor Bartomeu Robert, a former mayor of the city; a small, loose-skinned citrus fruit, usually with red-orange skin; and a film whose main characters are Rick Blaine and Ilse Lund?

4. Christopher Hitchens related how, in a collection of Irish writings, there is a 'wonderfully strict' correction of Louis MacNeice's translation of which two words as 'Ourselves Alone'? Hitchens continues, 'This is too common a mistake. The words mean "We Ourselves". I cannot think how such an important literal translation, with all its ironic implications, took so long to be made.'

5. Kamila Shamsie was nicknamed 'Nostrashamsie' by a friend after the first Muslim to occupy which position was appointed, the same position occupied by the Muslim character Karamat Lone in a 2017 novel by Shamsie? Other fictional occupants of this position include Julia Montague, portrayed on television by Keeley Hawes.

6. Who in 2005 broke a world record previously held by Francis Joyon and later that year became the youngest woman in modern history to be named a dame?

7. What does each of these words or names have in common with the others: a film based on a true story starring Ruth Negga and Joel Edgerton as a couple battling

* Not including Gladwyn Jebb, who was acting UN Secretary-General in 1945–6.

anti-miscegenation laws, the surname of the first woman to be appointed Commissioner of the Metropolitan Police Service, a TV series whose title characters are Hannah, Marnie, Jessa and Shoshanna, and the SI unit of inductance?

8. Who was announced as Sporting Equals Sportsman of the Year at the 2020 British Ethnic Diversity Sports Awards? In 2015 he moved to England, which he became eligible to represent in 2019 after the ECB changed their residency rules.

9. **Which stone creatures is it safe to return to life?**

The Silver Sorceress appears from behind a pillar and holds a dagger to Erick's throat. 'Didn't expect that, did you, Su Samuru?' she sneers. 'Call yourself an otter? More like. . . a rotter!' She high-fives the nearest stone creature.

'Spare him!' says Su Samuru. 'I will lay down my life in exchange for his. In the name of the deep magic, I reserve the right to—'

Before Su Samuru can finish his sentence, the Silver Sorceress stabs him through the heart and runs away, cackling.

The four siblings fall to their knees, weeping beside the body of the magnificent little otter – who stands up, unharmed.

'How on earth did you do that?' gasps Erick.

But the otter merely mutters something to Pedro, then exclaims, 'Now we go to Rio! An item sold there will help Pedro defeat Ethelbert, the ice-skating wolf, at the Pyramid of Fenris.'

'What? M-me? Ethelbert?' Pedro gurgles.

'The products at the stall are imported from Merrinmoor and labelled in the Merrinmoorean tongue,' continues Su Samuru. 'To give us a clue to which item to buy and how to use it, the stallholder will ask eight questions.'

It is a long, weary journey to Rio.

**Pedro, go to page 186.**
**All others, continue to the next page.**

## CHAPTER 4: ETHELBERT ATTACKS

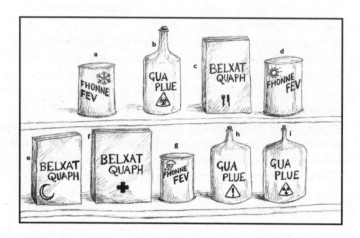

The stallholder asks the following questions:

1. A 2022 film in which John Mulaney and Andy Samberg voice chipmunks, a band who sparked the Riverport Riot in 1991 after leaving the stage in protest at 'the lame-ass security', and a Britney Spears single which was a cover of a song by the Arrows all contain what – though it is spelt with an apostrophe on the left, an apostrophe on the right and an apostrophe on either side respectively?

2. Which word is followed by an ellipsis to form the name of a cartoon strip, is followed by a dash to make a poem, an extract from which is inscribed above the players' entrance to Wimbledon's Centre Court, and appears without punctuation to make the name of songs by Pink Floyd and Janet Jackson?

3. An organization which describes itself as 'a lobbying coalition of trade and promotional associations and organizations actively involved in Wisconsin's tourism industry' changed its name to avoid being known by which letters,

whose NATO Phonetic Alphabet equivalents form the title of a 2016 film?

4. Which Belgian river gives its name to a 1914 battle in which the Belgians repelled a German offensive by flooding the land? In French, it is pronounced identically to the name of a river flowing through Grenoble.

5. Which Italian word, used in English as a musical direction, is an anagram of the surname of a man who was an Oscar nominee in 1992, 1999 and 2012 and is also an anagram of the first name of a man who was an Oscar winner in 1995 and 2020?

6. Ahmad Tibi, an Arab member of the Knesset, filed a police complaint after discovering that his image had been pasted on a what? In the film *Napoleon Dynamite*, an example of this object modelled on Summer Wheatly gets Pedro into trouble. A meat-filled example of this object was given to three tiger cubs at Whipsnade Zoo to celebrate their first birthday.

7. Which word should fill the blank in the following quotations? Firstly, from Shakespeare's *Measure for Measure*, 'Though music oft hath such a charm / To make bad good, and good _____ to harm', and secondly, from Thomas Gray's *Elegy Written in a Country Churchyard*, 'Can Honour's voice _____ the silent dust, / Or Flatt'ry soothe the dull cold ear of Death?'

8. Madalyn Murray O'Hair, described in a film title as 'The Most Hated Woman in America', founded an organization called American what? The organization's logo is an incomplete diagram of an atom, representing the fact that there is scientific knowledge yet to be discovered, with a capital A in its centre.

9. **Which item do you buy (give the appropriate letter) and how must Pedro use it to defeat Ethelbert?**

## CHAPTER 5: THE ROUT

Ethelbert is beaten. Su Samuru leads you all to Clig Fipper.

'This is where the final battle will occur!' exclaims Mrs Beaver.

'The Rout!' adds Mr Beaver. 'That's what the prophecy calls it.'

Su Samuru points to words carved into an ancient tree stump.

'Now, be savvy like a fox! Decode the ancient quiz-song! Jump to it!' exclaims the majestic little otter. Upon the stump these words are carved:

> *A group which inspired four mice*
> *Is to this song as The Rout*
> *Is to the conquering shout –*
> *With the otter's lost letter in, twice.*

'I'll ask the questions!' squeaks Mrs Beaver. 'I know what they'll be because I know the ancient prophecy by heart! Once the humans know the answers, they'll be able to figure out what the secret word is, which was conceived together with the deepest magic from before the dawn of time, and which, when shouted at the Sorceress, will conquer her and all her minions in an instant!'

She proceeds to recite:

1. Which word is the name of a Marvel Comics character who gains his powers from being tattooed by a mutant, and is also the name of a substance used in a test which inspired the name of a DC Comics character?

2. The names (in English) of an event in which Gregor Strasser was among those killed and an event two years later, whose winner described the man ultimately responsible for the first event as 'a man of dignity', both include which adjective, which is also the surname of the runner-up in the second event?

3. In an episode of *The Simpsons*, Mrs Krabappel puts on a short film whose protagonist has a nightmare that he

is living without what, the penultimate of its kind in alphabetical order? The name of this substance and two consecutive words found within this question combine to form an anagram of the name of a brand of vermouth.

4. Which surname may be followed by 'Medal' to make an accolade whose recipients include Thomas Henry Huxley and Francis Galton, or by 'Award' to make an accolade whose recipients include a man killed by accidentally triggering his own booby-trap?

5. What is the name of both a unit of length and a character described in the prologue to *The Wind Waker* as 'a young boy clothed in green'?

6. Gustaf Dalén, winner of the Nobel Prize in Physics for 'invention of automatic regulators for use in conjunction with gas accumulators for illuminating lighthouses and buoys', invented a product known by which three-letter name, the namesake of the company which originally manufactured it? He devised it after noticing that the burden of cooking was exhausting for his wife.

7. Which word should follow 'Mr' to make a fictional character formerly known as Lord Darlington or should follow 'The Great' to make a crisis which was alleviated by the ancestor of a former chairman of Endemol UK?

8. Which word, meaning 'pointed projection', is the name of a band whose songs include 'Snap Your Fingers, Snap Your Neck'? When pluralized, the word becomes the nickname of Harry Potter's father.

9. Which word is shared in the titles of a Bob Dylan song beginning, 'Well it ain't no use to sit and wonder why, babe' and a TV programme, one of whose episodes featured Danny Dyer discovering that he was descended from Edward III?

10. **The Silver Sorceress appears upon the horizon at the head of a huge army. They charge towards you with blood-curdling shrieks. What is the secret word which must be shouted to fell the army and win the battle?**   ⑤③

**Pedro, go to page 188.**
**All others, your quest is over.**

Silly old Pedro, Sadie and Lakrisha shouldn't get to share my Buddha's delight, you start thinking to yourself as the Beavers recite questions. They don't *deserve* to see a beautiful castle – they're happy hanging out with stinky beavers in their stinky beaver hut anyway.

You are resolved to set out alone.

**Between which two questions in the previous round have you sneaked off unnoticed?**

You are tired and hungry by the time you reach the castle.

'But where are your sister and brothers?' asks the lady. 'I am so very keen to meet them.'

You begin to explain that Pedro, Sadie and Lakrisha are too silly to be worthy of meeting her, but you trail off as she trembles with fury. A jet of white light crackles from her hand and envelops you. You cannot move. Your mind fogs up and the moisture vanishes from your body. This is the last thing you remember until. . .

You can move once more. An otter is standing before you. In the past, you would shave otters and draw grotesque images on their bodies without a moment's remorse, but now you are ashamed and cannot meet his gaze. You have a sneaking suspicion that the lady who turned you to stone is none other than the Silver Sorceress. Pedro, Sadie, Lakrisha and the Beavers are beside the otter. A faun – presumably Mr Ringo – is prancing exuberantly. Laid out upon the tiles are more stone creatures.

**Go to page 174.**

After you have walked for many hours, you hear rustling from a bush. A diminutive otter emerges. It strides towards you with an air of conviction, and you realize that you are in the presence of Su Samuru himself.

'Welcome, children,' he intones grandly. 'It is I, the true ruler of Mevania.'

'*You're* Su Samuru?' gasps Lakrisha. 'I thought you'd be a lion.'

'A *lion*? Why on earth would I be a lion?'

'Well,' you say, 'there was this note with lions hidden in it.' You are about to add that the fridge had the words 'LION WITHIN' written inside as well, but the otter looks increasingly agitated and you hold your tongue.

'So? I once did a jigsaw that had a picture of a slug. Did I decide that a completely random person was a slug? No, 'cause I'm not a big prat!'

'Your majesty,' cuts in Pedro hastily, 'truly, it is an honour—'

'A *lion* as king of Mevania – I ask you! It would have ripped your faces off as soon as look at you. You wouldn't have time to kneel before it because it would have gobbled up your knees! Very regal behaviour, *I don't think*!'

The otter is breathing heavily now and takes a minute to calm down. Then he announces in a deep, imposing voice, 'The Silver Sorceress has turned your brother to stone. Tomorrow we must save him. Tonight we rest.'

It is growing dark. With an authoritative little paw, he motions you towards a little hollow beside the road.

You awake to the sound of sleigh bells. Is it the Silver Sorceress advancing towards you? No! It's a Christmas elf. He has two gifts for you.

'Now is the time to use this weapon, Sadie,' the elf tells you. 'For an enchantress is spying on us, and will soon reveal our hiding place to the Silver Sorceress. Where can you find a name for what you have now become, and where can you find what to aim for?'

Shoot straight! **What is the name of the enchantress you impale?** ㊷

The horn the elf gives you is accompanied by a poem on a scrap of paper. It reads:

> *'If you chance on a shank or what's worn at its end*
> *Or a mass of small droplets or emerald hue,*
> *Blow on this horn – it will reap dividends,*
> *For there will be points that come drifting to you.*

'Blow this horn,' he continues, 'when you encounter four answers, all from the same round.'

**Which four answers make you blow your horn?** (Bear this in mind and return to this question later.) ㊷

The following day Su Samuru takes you to the Sorceress's castle. He extends a paw towards the stone figures of Erick and Mr Ringo, a sound emerges like the tinkling of a harp, and they spring into life – Mr Ringo exuberant and Erick shamefaced. Laid out upon the tiles are more stone creatures.

**Go to page 174.**

After you have walked for many hours, you hear rustling from a bush. A diminutive otter emerges. It strides towards you with an air of conviction, and you realize that you are in the presence of Su Samuru himself.

'Welcome, children,' he intones grandly. 'It is I, the true ruler of Mevania.'

'*You're* Su Samuru?' gasps Lakrisha. 'I thought you'd be a lion.'

'A *lion*? Why on earth would I be a lion?'

'Well,' says Sadie, 'there was this note with lions hidden in it.'

'So? I once did a jigsaw that had a picture of a slug. Did I decide that a completely random person was a slug? No, 'cause I'm not a big prat!'

'Your majesty,' you cut in hastily, 'truly, it is an honour—'

'A *lion* as king of Mevania – I ask you! It would have ripped your faces off as soon as look at you. You wouldn't have time to kneel before it because it would have gobbled up your knees! Very regal behaviour, *I don't think*!'

The otter is breathing heavily now and takes a minute to calm down. Then he announces in a deep, imposing voice, 'The Silver Sorceress has turned your brother to stone. Tomorrow we must save him. Tonight we rest.'

It is growing dark. With an authoritative little paw, he motions you towards a little hollow beside the road.

You awake to the sound of sleigh bells. Is it the Silver Sorceress advancing towards you? No! It's a Christmas elf. He has a gift for you: a pair of Dame Edna-style spectacles.

'These will allow you to see different things at once, and to reveal the secrets within the souls of beasts,' he explains.

The following day Su Samuru takes you to the Sorceress's castle. He extends a paw towards the stone figures of Erick and Mr Ringo, a sound emerges like the tinkling of a harp, and they spring into life – Mr Ringo exuberant and Erick shamefaced. Laid out upon the tiles are more stone creatures.

**Go to page 174.**

# PEDRO

This is what Su Samuru had muttered to you at the castle:

'Put on your glasses, Pedro.'

Curiously, the stone creatures now appear superimposed upon the map of Mevania. 'What secret do the wicked conceal?'

**What message is revealed, which is as close as you're going to get to an explanation of how Su Samuru has been resurrected?** 53

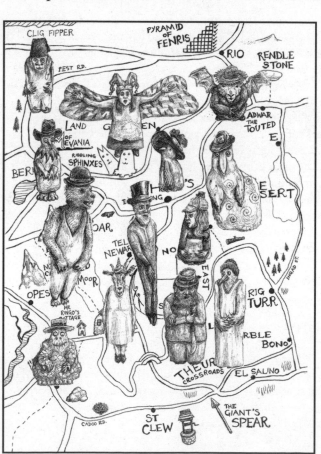

Now Su Samuru leans close to you. 'Do not be afraid, Pedro. You remind me of a boy named Peter, who was also pitted against a ferocious wolf and came away victorious.'

'You mean, in *The Lion, the Witch and the Wardrobe*?'

'The which, the who and the what? What you said makes no sense at all. No, two answers from the next round form an anagram. This will tell you what I'm thinking of.'

**Which two answers does Su Samuru mean?** (You'll need to come back to this question.) ㊷

**Go to page 178.**

The battle has ended. You and your siblings are crowned kings and queens of Mevania. 'How will my reign be remembered?' you ask Su Samuru.

'They will call you,' responds the otter, 'King Pedro the. . .'

'Yes?'

'Take that which turns dark blue into a manual labourer. Follow it with an answer from the last chapter, which could have been listed among the examples used in a much earlier question. An answer from the last chapter is the capital of the end of this word. **What is this eleven-letter word by which you will be known?'**

**Your quest is over.**

# EPILOGUE

*Hints on page 215*

*Answers on page 271*

A chill wind blows as howling spirits reel around you and disappear with a flash and a crackle. Stars in the distance flicker and fade. It is as if all is cowering in the presence of something immensely powerful. Milbert appears beside you.

'We've done it, Milbert!' you exclaim in a weak attempt at triumph. 'Haven't we?' You reach to high-five him. His hands remain tightly clasped.

'I don't know, Miss Quincunx. No-one has ever got this far. I thought it would end now. . . but there's *something* out here. It's stopping us from going any further. Don't you feel it?'

A figure shrouded in a huge cloak drifts towards you. It is reading *A DRAMATIC ENDING & how to build up to it*, which it suddenly tosses into the void. Its face remains unseen. It reminds you of the Ghost of Christmas Yet to Come, but fills you with such an unearthly chill that it makes the Ghost of Christmas Yet to Come seem as unthreatening as Winnie-the-Pooh with his head stuck in a honey jar. It spreads gloved hands wide apart, stretching a silken screen between them. The screen shows Jim, desperate and alone, pounding like a mime at the invisible borders of your old dimension. 'Jim!' gasps Milbert. He darts towards the figure, which snaps its hands shut. The screen vanishes in a cascade of dust. Milbert backs away.

In a deep, rattling voice, the figure says: 'Jim's soul is mine, just as all souls that are lost without hope are mine. He will work for me and you will never save him. Never – unless you tell me who I am.' It proceeds to ask these questions:

1. Which first name is shared by a sprinter who won three gold medals at the 1960 Summer Olympics, the first woman to be Principal Chief of the Cherokee Nation and a fictional character whose maiden name is the subject of a continuity error, initially being Pebble and later referred to as Slaghoople?

2. A word meaning 'relaxes' may be divided into two unequal parts: the first may follow four letters to mean 'cover with trees again'; the second may follow three letters to mean 'swear'. The four letters followed by the three letters spell out which word, which fills in the blank in this quotation from Barack Obama: 'I promised to _____ on the terrorists who actually attacked us on 9/11. We have'?

3. A material found in tusks, a variety of beryl coloured by chromium (or sometimes vanadium), fresh air, and precipitation during the warmest season are likened to various features and qualities of a fictional character, who was inspired by a real-life bank teller. She is arguably the most famous character created by which person?

4. Which word fills the first blank space in this extract from the introduction to a 2020 interview with Armenian Prime Minister Nikol Pashinyan in the *Spectator*? The twelve-letter word that fills the second blank space is one of the few that rhyme with this word.

   *Russia _____ backs Armenia, while also selling arms to Azerbaijan, and Turkey supports Azerbaijan.*
   *Dozens of civilians have already been killed in the new round of fighting that began on Sunday. Armenia, once the clear superior, is now confronting a _____ well-equipped rival.*

5. 'Visual representations', 'piece of music performed by two people' and 'working as a sleeper agent' are definitions of words and phrases which form the names of versions of what? The latter version includes 'UDDERS', 'ORGY' and 'WHIP'.

6. Take the first name and middle initial of 'Bucky' Barnes, a character (apparently) named after a political leader whose

obituary in the *Chicago Tribune* stated, 'This desolate old man has gone to his grave. No son or daughter is doomed to acknowledge an ancestry from him'. Barnes is associated with a group which shares its name with a TV series which ran from 1961 to 1969; take the surname of the most prominent male character in this 1960s series. Barnes appears in a film franchise; give the final word of the title of the 2008 film which began Phase One of this franchise. You have spelt out the name of which major-general during the American Civil War?

7. What name is given to a public holiday celebrated in the Australian Capital Territory, which Dr Tjanara Goreng Goreng of the University of Canberra described as 'a celebration of the First Nations people in this area; their diversity, their capabilities, their services'? It is also the name of a holiday observed in South Africa since 1995 on 16 December, though this holiday is more commonly known with the two words swapped round and the word 'of' placed between them.

8. Which first name is shared by characters responsible for the deaths of a real-estate secretary who steals $40,000 and of the daughter of the NYPD captain George Stacy, having thrown her from a bridge (though in one film adaptation, this man's son Harry is depicted as the murderer instead)?

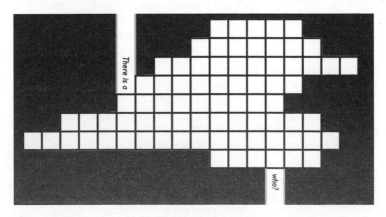

'Look at this grid, Infinity,' says the figure. 'Confusing, isn't it? Which are the paths and which are the walls? Find one dimension whose name contains all the letters of the name of another dimension – but beware a red herring. In the former dimension, a seven-word phrase leads you to your final answers. In the latter, one answer secures a climactic victory. If you translate the seven words literally to make seven French words, all their letters but one are walls. All but two letters of the word from the second dimension are paths. The three letters which are the odd ones out spell something which you must not do when you answer this, if you are to have any hope of seeing Jim again. Take the quickest route through the grid, and answer the question.'

**What, according to the mysterious figure, must you not do when answering the question in the grid?**

**What is the answer to the question in the grid?** 64

'So *that's* who you are!' you gasp. 'I might have known!'
   'Au contraire, Infinity. Heed the beginnings of what lie between the dimensions.'

**Who is the mysterious figure *really*?** 42

'*No!*' shrieks the mysterious figure. 'Why did I feel compelled to give you those clues?'

The darkness is rent asunder and the figure whimpers and whirls away as dazzling light floods through. Visions from previous quizzes parade past you – a dog with a slight resemblance to Adam West, old Juke Limburger red in the face as he belts out his nonsensical song, a menacing pair of lovebirds, close behind them the sneaky, tittering Grod, Professor Mariachi, thirteen howling demons, a meerkat snarling with each of her seven heads, ten-foot-tall crows armed to the beaks, a pizza bursting into flames, an ocean wave bearing fragments of castle walls, a helicopter, and the Silver Sorceress upon a sleigh. Now they are gone and all is vast, luminous emptiness.

You make out a small bouncy castle floating towards you. As it draws closer, you hear a listless cover of 'The Girl from Ipanema' playing from a tinny speaker.

'Welcome to Who Dares Wings, the place where wings are available to those who have earned them,' mutters the proprietor, her eyes fixed on her magazine, as she constantly adjusts her footing to prevent the stool she is sitting on from overbalancing on the wobbly floor. 'No time-wasters, please.'

'Angelic greetings to you! My name, madam, is Milbert Cardew. This is my underling; she answers to the name of Miss Quincunx, though you may call her Infinity. We have. . . done the dozen.'

The proprietor falls off her stool. 'The Girl from Ipanema' stops abruptly; over the speaker, you hear musicians dropping their instruments and the singer yelling out, '*What?*'

The proprietor darts into a back room and emerges staggering under the weight of a huge, glistening pair of feathery wings. She releases them and they soar through the air and alight on Milbert's back.

Milbert shrieks with childish delight. He turns a loop-the-loop. 'Wings!' he exclaims. 'Milbert Cardew is an angel with *wings*! And they're spectacular!' He soars away without a goodbye, without a backward glance. A minute later, he returns with a shell-shocked Jim clinging limply to him.

'Can I go home now, Milbert?' he murmurs. 'I've learnt my lesson now, I promise! That angelic punishment was harsher than I imagined.'

'Oh, Jim, it's all my fault. I'm supposed to be your guardian angel and you'd have been better off with a garden snail. I know you want to go home, but you can't. You remember Miss Quincunx, don't you, who was supposed to jump off the bridge? Well, instead of drowning, she corrupted your whole reality.'

'Oh,' says Jim weakly. 'Hello, Infinity.'

'I did helpful stuff too,' you point out.

'Oh, yes, certainly,' says Milbert hastily. 'I didn't mean to suggest it would have been better if you'd drowned. We can never really know the consequences of things, can we? A butterfly flaps its wings in China and all of a sudden London Bridge falls down, or some such. Anyway, Jim, I've got a lovely dimension waiting for you with a sunny beach, like the ones in the posters you kept in your room. Two deckchairs side by side. Speaking of which, I could do with a little sit-down myself. What do you say, old buddy?'

'Fine,' mumbles Jim, who looks so addled that you suspect he'd have responded the same way if Milbert had promised him a year's stay glued to the inside of a factory chimney.

Milbert carries Jim into the distance.

'Hey!' you bellow. '*HEY!*'

He turns back.

'Ah, Miss Quincunx, it was rude of me – in my excitement I forgot to say goodbye. And, Miss Quincunx, I *am* grateful for your help.'

'But what do I do now?'

'Oh! I must say, I hadn't given the matter much thought.'

You restrain the urge to point out that you've brought up the subject before.

'I suppose, of course,' muses Milbert, 'I could obliterate you. You are my creation after all.'

'*After all I've done for you, you prat-face?*'

'It was merely a suggestion. But if it doesn't appeal. . . Oh, I have just the role for you! My colleague has an assignment in a couple of months. It's Hound-Grog Day then, when intoxicated dogs predict the weather with the texture of their vomit. There's a cynical man who relives the day over and over. At one point he seduces a woman who refers to parts of her body as if they were items on a fast-food menu, a habit so crass that it makes him realize that his sweet, idealistic colleague has been his true love all along. You'd be perfect for the fast-food debauchee! We'd have to wipe your memory, of course, but it'd be a good chance to forget your past. . . no? Well, I'm afraid I'm out of ideas.'

'How did you get to be a Christmas angel?' you venture. 'Could I. . .?'

'A Christmas angel?' gasps Milbert, nearly dropping Jim in shock. 'Oh, but it took decades of training! Exams upon exams! Zorbing in giant but extremely fragile baubles and balancing on the top of terrifyingly high Christmas trees. And when I started, I was a fairly respectable. . . well, anyway, the Christmassy stories are all resolved now. There'd be nowhere for you to—'

With the sound of an invisible choir, a hazy orb appears and grows larger before your eyes. 'Help us, please!' announces a wide-eyed young girl within. 'Our beloved department store Father Christmas has been taken to court, where he and his rival Father Christmases must be interrogated in a baffling logic puzzle!'

'A new dimension – out of nowhere!' cries Milbert. 'But it's impossible!'

'When you've done the dozen, Infinity,' says the proprietor, 'all things are possible. Come on, angel, let's get you your wings.'

'*Wings*?' burbles Milbert. 'She gets wings a literal *ten seconds* after saying she wants to be an angel? But look at her! Well. . . strike me down!' He looks around nervously, as if worried that this request might be taken literally.

The proprietor beckons you into the shop. You look back at Milbert.

'Miss Quincunx. . . Infinity, I should say,' he says. 'I'm proud of you. Well done.'

It sounds patronizing and slightly insincere, but it's the best you can hope for from Milbert. You smile at him. He returns the smile bemusedly, still shaking his head in disbelief.

You go into the shop to get your wings.

These tattered wings frequently stop working and the angels who run the helpline are deliberately obtuse.

**75 points**

The striking appearance of these stone wings almost makes up for what they lack in practicality. Comes with a set of plasters inadequate to heal all the body parts you'll be spraining.

**130 points**

These fluffy little wings have a single special feature: the ability to spray filth when you press a button marked 'Befoul'.

**260 points**

These ultra-sleek wings will carry you with the greatest of ease. Warning: after frequent use, these wings develop a slight aroma of turbot.

**380 points**

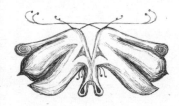

These extraordinary wings come with an array of special features – simply pick up the controller and scroll through its menus!

**500 points**

These super-deluxe, jewel-encrusted wings are jet-propelled thanks to Clu-Hat technology. The vast array of special features includes an extendable arm which dangles marshmallows into your mouth as you fly and a selection of weapons such as spikes tipped with poison.

**600 points**

This masterpiece of modern wing design comes with features beyond the wildest dreams of the wildest characters in your wildest dreams. As you soar at unprecedented speeds, immerse yourself in a world of entertainment, vanquish your enemies in a huge variety of ways or simply terrify them by using the light beams to project the image of a huntsman.

**715 points**

# HINTS

# IT'S A WONDERFUL MULTIVERSE

**The colours**

How do the answers to the Satan Crater's trivia night differ from those of the Prudent Clergyman's trivia night?

# A CHRISTMAS KRILL

**How do you ensure that your dog is the winner?**

The ink turns 'Mind-bending master plan' into 'Bind-mending plaster man'. What must you use it on to ensure that no dog but yours can be pronounced the winner?

**Which four shapes form the combination to the Clogitts' chest of drawers?**

Look at your answers to Julia Clogitt's questions – specifically, their endings and beginnings.

**There is something you must do before you return to the future. In the future, you must ensure that you will be able to open the Clogitts' wall compartment when you go back to the present, so you can recover your humbugs. What course of action do you take?**

First, you must perform an act in the present which changes the sculpture in the future. This will enable you to replicate a part of Bogg's anatomy. The next step is within plain sight; after that, you will be equipped to return to the present and open the compartment.

# LOVE, FACTUALLY

**In which position does each word go in Juke Limburger's song?**

The words in positions 1, 9 and 14 begin and end in the same letter. The only evenly numbered word not to have seven letters occupies position 12.

**Where is the man's destination?**

'Juke Limburger's advice' refers to the title of Juke Limburger's song. Go clockwise.

**What message do the cards spell, when arranged in numerical order?**

Cards 4, 6, 9, 13 and 14 have three letters on them.

**Which item would the chief of staff's girlfriend most appreciate from him?**

Jacques Necker was finance minister under Louis XVI. Leo XIII was Pope at the turn of the twentieth century.

**But which one is Carla?**

Take the first letters, followed by the last letters, from the last two rounds, which gives a message telling you to use Round 1 to find a further message. This further message tells you to look for five answers that have something in common – that thing being that they all have the same number of letters – and alter them in a certain way to produce the names of five of the six animals.

# THE CHRISTMAS BEFORE

**Who is Jim's special somebody, and which letter does his special somebody correspond to?**

Can B's statements both be false without contradicting each other? Thus, what can we deduce from F's claim to have written the card? And what can we then deduce from A agreeing with F that Mel is a liar (and E disagreeing), and from C's claim to be Sue?

# THE GROD WHO OBLITERATED CHRISTMAS

**Find the place on the map where your gifts are located –
Your holiday frolics may not be frustrated!**

Insert *URTSHFOHEFFUPLNGR*, the first letters of each line on the previous page, into these seven answers to spell the message.

**Are you out of the maze? Is your brain overloaded?
Tell me the message that you have decoded.**

Tupac Shakur and Gisele Bündchen* are among those depicted on the sheets you must cross.

**Which Venns, if they heeded their lust to unwrap
Irresistible gifts, would be caught in my trap?**

They are both female Venns with the same number of letters in their names.

**So those are the questions – you've had time to read 'em.
What is the island that leads you to freedom?**

The answers to this round correspond to the layout of Vennburg. Chickering & Sons was a piano manufacturer. The correct answer may call to mind a British TV chef.

.........................................................................

\* Although Gisele Bündchen's forename is frequently pronounced 'Zhiz-ell' outside Brazil, it's the Brazilian pronunciation of 'Zhiz-ellie' that will help you here. (Thanks to Alex Furby for his Portuguese expertise and thorough research into this topic!)

# SHERBERT HICKS AND THE BLUE GARFUNKEL

## Who left the note?

The unaccounted-for words in the note can be rearranged to make the name of the establishment which this man runs.

## To which building is the sculpture being taken?

The answers to the previous questions have the same initials as locations on the map, which can be traversed, in order, starting from the En Den. What is omitted in the names of these locations? Once you have figured out the message, you must discover from other parts of the quiz where the person mentioned lives.

## What is the hidden message describing the effect of Serum 2?

Find words in the newspaper immediately above names of seas.

## What is the hidden message describing the effect of Serum 3?

Find words in the newspaper immediately to the right of synonyms for 'reply'.

## What is the hidden message describing the effect of Serum 4?

Find words in the newspaper immediately below synonyms for 'zero' ('O' is not among those synonyms). This will give you a longer sentence than either of the previous two and includes sporting synonyms for 'zero'.

## Which building must you head for now?

From the answers gleaned from the sera and assignments, take the first letter of the first, the second letter of the second, etc. Look at the location of each person or place on the map; it is significant that the map is divided into a 3 x 3 grid.

**In which container are the sculpted Simon and Garfunkel?**

Each description of an item in the list of sculptures includes a gift given on one of the twelve days of Christmas (the fact that some gifts mentioned in the song have not been included in the list is not significant); each description also contains a single letter *i*. Drawing on the page (or on a copy of it, if you prefer) may prove useful.

# THE GIFT ON THE
# THIRTEENTH DAY

**Driving out the demons**

1. The four words you must remove all have four letters and may be found more than once in the answers.
2. In Round 1, the last four letters of one answer are first four of the next, except for the end of one answer and the beginning of the next. What do they spell out?
3. Round 1 contains 'A' 'E' 'I' and 'U' as separate words – but not 'O'. Find other words that fit this pattern (such as, say, 'blander', 'blender', 'blinder' and 'blunder') and piece together the film's title from the missing ones.
4. Look for two boxers who contested a famous fight.
5. The initial letters of answers to Round 3 spell out what you need.
6. The first and last answers whose final letter you remove are linked (in the questions) by the same TV programme.
7. The answer I'm looking for ends in the same six letters as one of Round 1's answers.
8. I'm looking for Shakespeare characters; three of them are title characters of plays.
9. The answer to Round 3, Question 7, is what you must change.
10. To begin with, find answers which share the letters 'loner'. The answer I'm looking for once said, 'Making money is art, and working is art and good business is the best art.'
11. Look for homophones of Roman numerals, then seek two five-letter answers and remove the first two letters from one of these answers.
12. All of the answers in one round, when taken as a single string of letters and spelt backwards, are other answers in this quiz – with one exception.
13. Find three-letter strings shared within trios of answers.
14. Find letters to change in an author, members of a profession, a city and a sign before you reach the letter which must be added to wine.

# THE NUT-KRAKEN

**Which item in the playroom moves diagonally down and right and which one moves diagonally down and left?**

In reordering the lines of the letter (you don't need to rearrange the words within them, just change the order of the lines themselves), look for lines which conclude with a fragment ending in a hyphen, which can combine with the beginnings of other lines to form new words.

**What are the four answers in the grid that tell you which pieces you must move and how you must move them?**

The second crossword can be 'built' out of the first crossword by rearranging the 3x3 squares it is made up of (including the letters that should be contained in those 3x3 squares). These 3x3 squares must not be rotated. The letters in the four unclued answers you seek can be made by working out which squares in the first crossword they correspond to.

**What is the final message, which tells you what to move and how, so that the wicked creature's muddles and messes can be undone forever?**

The six items move one square at a time, except for the jumping one, which moves directly from the square before the jumpable object to the one after it. 'Jump the snake' is not an idiom, or at least not one I'm familiar with. When movable items (and remember, this applies only to *movable* items) occupy the same space, return to Dieselmotor's letter and find a string of letters *of the same length as the number of the grid reference*, which occur *between two instances of the same letter found in the grid reference*. None of these strings of letters is spread across more than one line (which is why it does not matter whether or not you use the rearranged version), and they spell out the final message when taken in the order corresponding to the order in which the spaces are landed on.

# THE CROW MAN

**Joining the letters and numbers in the book**

Find pairs of letters, or pairs consisting of a letter and a number, which form homophones of words indicated by the book's symbols. The symbol above the crystal ball indicates a word meaning 'have prescience of'.

**The magic word**

Look for what is missing from each line.

**The map**

Find the only words on the map that correspond to the location of the tick.

**The crows' mysterious diagram**

The chief crow is showing a word ladder with two entries missing. Beneath it, the footprints represent different letters used in the word ladder.

**The war**

The answer is an anagram of the previous answers, plus the letter and number seen on the sole of the crop-trampler's boot. The lines indicate where the letters of each answer fit into the anagram, which will help you in identifying the year.

# THE BOY WHO LIVED BY HIMSELF

**Which two steps will harmlessly turn the TV on and off?**

Words concealed horizontally in the grid form the outline of steps.

**Now, what's my secret, boys?**

The introduction forms an acrostic guiding you to three words. Kevin McCallister, the protagonist of *Home Alone*, is Genghis's hero.

**In what order do you arrange them?**

Those in places 3, 4 and 5 are verbs which are synonyms. Those in places 7, 8 and 9 are tracks on the same album. The connection between 13, 14 and 15 relates to the spelling and pronunciation of the words.

**What number do you dial?**

Look for a name, a pronoun, a word meaning 'resound' and a word denoting a person unlikely to be referred to by the aforementioned pronoun.

**Which pizza do you order?**

Phrases meaning 'period of environmental devastation following a conflict' and 'Asian delicacy' can be made when you replace the first two objects.

**You type a password. What do you type?**

The number of times an ingredient appears on each slice corresponds to a letter of that ingredient's name.

**In which grid reference do you find the Von Millicent fortune?**

The dining room's round refers to the line in Genghis's poem 'I can't believe she reduced the bout to ants!'; this is how you must treat the answers to the final round.

**In which grid reference do you find the only safe exit?**

Reverend Snakes's advice is to 'start from scratch'. Merv is scratching himself – where do you reach if you start from there and continue in the direction of each arrow you encounter?

# GOOD QUEEN WESSELSBRON

### The meeting place

Three adjectives found in the lyrics to the carol which inspired this round will help you. Some of the films are better known than others but their titles are recognizable phrases in their own right.

### The game

The pockets of letters formed are bordered only by the brands found diagonally, never by the edges of the grid. The letters in the two pockets can be read left to right, top to bottom, to spell out the game.

### The creature's identity

You must take the even letters of six-letter answers to make three-letter words, names and acronyms. Find trios of words found within the questions which define them. In the case of the two acronyms, these trios are simply what the acronym stands for; in another case, the trio consists of three synonyms of the three-letter word. If the second words of each trio are arranged in the order in which they occur in the questions, they spell out a name commonly given to a type of building.


# DIE, HARDLY

**What does the terrorist plan to harness, in order to unleash it and destroy the world?**

Til implies, when she says, 'Get to the heart of every answer', that you must take the middle three letters of every answer; these spell a message telling you how to find another message. This second message spells out three further questions. The first of these questions should be answered with an abbreviation. The second of these questions must be answered with the help of the calendar and the words of those you have spoken to so far. Respace the letters of your three answers to find the phrase you need.

**What is the hidden message of Round 2, which will help you work out the terrorist's identity?**

Different words may follow the answers in Round 2 so that they match the books in Til's pile; starting from the word following the final answer, read these words backwards.

**Who is the terrorist?**

The display must be altered in a certain way. Check the calendar before you conclude who the culprit is!

**What is the hidden message of this round, which instigates an uproar among the hostages?**

The last two answers of Round 3 are the names of bands with the final *s* removed. The answers to Questions 5 and 7 must have the second word of what the terrorist plans to harness added, while the others must have it removed. You are exposing an extramarital affair.

**What is the four-digit combination?**

The answers to Round 3 must be entered into a grid as depicted in the room containing the 'Obe Babe'. The propellor contains the letters CLU HAT, such that the propellor can be moved into a different position to alter the words in the grid. The shapes that the propellor makes in order to alter each word are significant.

**What is the hidden message?**

Decode the message to the left of the safe – it is no coincidence that the building has twenty-six windows. Each answer in Round 5 corresponds to an item in the roof plan; the path you must take between them has been depicted previously. The instructions will tell you which letters of each answer to use. The message's final five letters are not nonsense but initials.

# INTO THE FRIDGE

## SADIE

### The fridge's message

This message can be spelt out by rearranging (without anagramming) the fridge's contents. ·

## ERICK

### The thought that worms its way into your head

What happens when you join up the lines within the stars?

### The directions to the castle

Find two 'delights' on the map; what is missing from the quickest route between them?

## CHAPTER 2: THE DISAPPEARANCE OF ERICK

### In which direction must Pedro, Sadie, Lakrisha and the Beavers go to find Su Samuru and avoid the Sorceress's minions?

Find letters that occur the same number of times, in total, within this chapter's previous answers.

## LAKRISHA

### The message of reassurance

Find answers that can be prefixed with Mr Ringo's tune.

### Shading by numbers

Which word could precede all of those underlined in the note?

### The message leading to the final object

The numbers mentioned in the second item's description refer to chapter numbers and question numbers. The fourth word of the second item's description is used in the same sense in which it is used in cryptic crosswords.

**ALL**

## CHAPTER 3: AT THE SORCERESS'S CASTLE

### Question 9

The previous answers relate to what is worn by creatures who will do you no harm.

**ALL**

## CHAPTER 4: ETHELBERT ATTACKS

### Question 9

Look at the Pyramid of Fenris on the map. Start by inserting your answers vertically into the grid.

**ALL**

## CHAPTER 5: THE ROUT

### Question 10

The 'group which inspired four mice' has appeared earlier. What is the rhyme scheme of the poem beginning, '*A group which inspired four mice*'?

**ERICK**

Look back to the Sorceress's advice and apply it to Chapter 2.

**SADIE**

### The enchantress you impale with your arrow

Look at the card the Professor gave you. Its dots correspond to questions in the chapters of this quiz. Find two significant answers – what letters does your arrow cross?

213

### When to blow your horn

Find words that may precede the word 'horn' to make new words; these four answers consist of two rhyming pairs (although the rhyming words do not appear consecutively).

PEDRO

### The secret that the wicked conceal

What do the wicked animals conceal on the map when Pedro looks through his Dame Edna glasses?

### Su Samuru's anagram

Look for two answers which collectively form an anagram of a composer's surname.

### How Pedro will be known

What does 'navy' need to become 'navvy'? I'm looking for a two-word answer, a five-letter word followed by a single letter. Find a palindrome. The last two letters are a two-letter abbreviation.

# EPILOGUE

**What, according to the mysterious figure, must you not do when answering the question in the grid?**

If '*Tous pour un et un pour tous*'* contains one odd one out, 'Support our troops' and 'Toy Story Two' contain none.

**What is the answer to the question in the grid?**

Thirteen may be walls, thirteen may be paths. The answer to the question has been mentioned in a previous question.

**Who is the mysterious figure *really*?**

The mysterious figure is alluding to the Winterludes.

- - - - - - - - - - - - - - - - - - - - - - - - - - - - - - - - - - - - - - - - - - -

\*    In Dumas's *The Three Musketeers*, the motto (which is mentioned only twice) appears as '*Tous pour un, un pour tous*'.

# ANSWERS

# IT'S A WONDERFUL MULTIVERSE

### The Satan Crater's trivia night:

1. Puri
2. Did [*I Know What You Did Last Summer* and 'Oops!. . . I Did It Again']
3. Land [Kathrine *Switzer*; *Po*; *Ice*; *Fin*]
4. Sing
5. Bing [Bing Crosby]*
6. Boom
7. Sling
8. Ruger [Justin Kruger]

### The Prudent Clergyman's trivia night:

1. Puritan
2. Disabled
3. Greenland
4. Screaming [Lord Sutch]
5. Plumbing
6. Boredom
7. Slumbering
8. Rulemonger

### The eight colours:

Tan; Sable; Green; Cream; Plum; Red; Umber; Lemon [The two trivia nights have answers spelt identically apart from the strings of letters spelling out colours.]

••••••••••••••••••••••••••••••••••••••••••••••••••••••••••••••••••••••••

\*   Crosby's nickname is more likely to have been inspired by his youthful love for the comic strip *The Bingville Bugle*.

# WINTERLUDE 1

1. Maida Vale [Made of ale]
2. Taipei [Type A]
3. New Delhi [Nude Ellie (Goulding)]
4. Winchester [Winch Esther (Rantzen)]
5. Munich [Mew, 'Nick!' (Cave)]
6. Algiers [Al jeers]
7. Southport [Sow thport]

# A CHRISTMAS KRILL

1. Costa [South Africa, United States of America, Costa Rica]
2. Repent
3. Agony uncle
4. Filthy lucre
5. Scent

**How do you ensure that your dog is the winner?**

The ink creates spoonerisms; pour it over the note reading 'Pot Noodles' to make it read 'Not Poodles' and place it in the slot.

**Which four shapes form the combination to the Clogitts' chest of drawers?**

Star; Pentagon; Clef; Crescent [The shapes' names are hidden in the answers to the quiz round, formed from the final letter or letters of one answer and the first letter or letters of the next.]

**There is something you must do before you return to the future. In the future, you must ensure that you will be able to open the Clogitts' wall compartment when you go back to the present, so you can recover your humbugs. What course of action do you take?**

Replace the photograph of Henry Kissinger with the photograph of Adam West from the canine lookalike contest; the sculpture in the future will now depict Adam West. In the future, place Bogg Clogitt's apple into the box underneath the sculpture, whereupon it becomes Bogg Clogitt's Adam's apple. Call Sgt Swoope's Swap Shop to have your own Adam's apple exchanged for Bogg Clogitt's. Return to the present and, using Bogg Clogitt's Adam's apple, open the voice-activated compartment in the wall.

# WINTERLUDE 2

*The Polar Express*

*White Christmas*

*Ernest Saves Christmas*

*Holiday Inn*

*Jingle All the Way*

*It's a Wonderful Life*

*The Muppet Christmas Carol*

*Babes in Toyland*

# LOVE, FACTUALLY

**In which position does each word go in Juke Limburger's song?**

1. summoners
2. aunties
3. serrated
4. czarism
5. confessor
6. echoing
7. tiddlers
8. movable
9. evidence
10. realism
11. lettuces
12. turbogenerated
13. backgammon
14. sickies
15. splaying
16. scissor

## Departures board

1. Sark* [Cutty Sark]
2. Le Havre [Minerva; Helen of Troy]
3. St Andrews [Shirley Temple and Julie Andrews]
4. El Nido [Leonid Brezhnev]
5. Isle of Man

....................................................................

\* André Gardes, who had put up posters announcing that his invasion would begin the following day at noon, was disarmed and arrested by the island's volunteer constable before the fateful hour arrived.

**Where is the man's destination?**

Arkhangelsk, flight code LTE [Juke Limburger's song is called 'Go Round the Big Hole', which serves as advice for this round: if you insert the destinations horizontally into the grid, the letters surrounding the large gap containing no letters read 'ARKHANGELSKLTE', starting from the top left and moving clockwise.]

**Double Questions**

1. If [*The*; *Thief*]
2. You [Wat; way out]
3. Hug [Skin; Husking]
4. Me [Blood (*Blood Sugar Sex Magik*, *First Blood*); Bloomed]
5. Again [I'm into; Imagination]
6. I [Deprecate; Depreciate]
7. Shall [Out (*Time Out*); (Neville) Southall]
8. Puke [Alle, Paul Klee]

**The cards**

1. Juju [Sundin; Smith-Schuster]
2. Holy day
3. Stepdad
4. Ureter
5. Mind Fist
6. Rout
7. Yo estoy
8. Outdid

**What message do the cards spell, when arranged in numerical order?**

'Do you mind if I say you're just utterly drop-dead hot?'

1. Incontinence pads
2. Neckerchief
3. Ski

4. Oar
5. Napoleons
6. Gold dust
7. Epaulettes
8. Ashtray

## Which item would the chief of staff's girlfriend most appreciate from him?

The ashtray

['This is a three-letter item of sporting equipment' applies to both 'ski' and 'oar'. 'What I'm describing begins with the name of an important political figure in French history who lived from the eighteenth to the early nineteenth century' applies to both '*napoleons*' and '*necker*chief' (Jacques Necker was finance minister under Louis XVI). 'What I'm describing contains the name of a metallic chemical element' applies to both '*gold* dust' and 'incon*tin*ence pads'. 'These items contain the papal name of a Roman Catholic pope who died during the twentieth century (though the name has also been used by earlier popes)' applies to both 'napo*leons*' and '*epaul*ettes'.]

1. Curl [Robert Curl won the Nobel Prize for co-discovering fullerenes]
2. Hannibal [Buress and Lecter]
3. Wanda
4. Oddjob
5. Rapunzel [*Tangled*]
6. Desire [*A Streetcar Named Desire*]

## But which one is Carla?

The frog.

[Carla's note advises you to take the first letters, followed by the last letters, from the last two rounds, giving the message 'In song, each word's first syllable'. The first syllables, in order, of each word in the song make up homophones of the message 'Some answers are connected; move every letter back six places'. The five connected answers are the only ones that, like the animals represented by the costumes, have four letters in total: Sark, Puke, Juju, Rout, Curl. If their letters are moved back six places (in the same way that, in the final round, the first letter of 'Wanda' can be moved back to make 'V and A', and if the alphabet is seen as a continuous loop where *a* minus 1 = *z*), they become 'Mule, Joey, Dodo, Lion, Wolf'.]

# WINTERLUDE 3

1. 'Hello, Goodbye'
2. 'Green, Green Grass of Home'
3. 'I Will Always Love You'
4. 'Return to Sender'
5. 'Moon River'
6. 'Sound of the Underground'
7. 'Another Brick in the Wall (Part Two)'
8. 'Earth Song'

# THE CHRISTMAS BEFORE

1. *Indiscreet* [Inn; diss; Crete]
2. *Enchanted* [Inch; aunt; id]
3. *Clueless*
4. *Lost in Translation*
5. *True Romance* [Truro; manse]
6. *Brief Encounter* [Brie fin counter]
7. *Bride Wars* [Braai; 'drawers' with a 'dw' sound instead of 'dr']

## Inside the card

1. Lamb [snar**l, amb**er]
2. Angel [c**lang, el**ement]
3. Dearest [wi**de are st**ring]
4. Babe [tu**ba, beg**ging]
5. Petal [ca**pe tal**ked]
6. Cutie [un**cut, I e**merged]
7. Honey [**shone y**our]

## Person A

1. Mel
2. Lies [*Big Little Lies*; *True Lies*]
3. She wrote ['That's All'; *Murder*]
4. To you ['To me, to you', the catchphrase of the Chuckle Brothers; 'From Me to You']
5. I am [*Legend*; *Sasha Fierce*]
6. Paul [Henri Paul (no relation); *Paul Clifford*]

## Person B

1. I Didn't Do It
2. A liar
3. Did [Did not finish]
4. It [*Five Children and It*; *It*]

**Person C**

1. My name is Sue
2. Simon says
3. Nothing but the truth

**Person D**

1. *Mel and Sue*
2. Can't write
3. I am not [*Why I Am Not a Christian*]
4. Simon [Paul ('50 Ways to Leave Your Lover') and Carly ('You're So Vain')]

**Person E**

1. *Paul is*
2. The Author
3. Mel [Tormé; Blanc]
4. Never Lies [*Tomorrow Never Dies*]
5. Sue [Bird]
6. Can write

**Person F**

1. I wrote
2. The card
3. I'm Not [*Whatever People Say I Am, That's What I'm Not; I'm Not There*]
4. Sue
5. Mel [Smith; Gibson; Brooks]
6. Lies ['Lies, damned lies and statistics']

**Who is Jim's special somebody, and which letter does his special somebody correspond to?**

Paul; C

[B cannot be the writer, because if 'I didn't do it' were false, 'A liar did it' would be true. B must be a truthteller as B's statements cannot both be false. F must be a liar, since we know from B that 'A liar did it' and F claims, 'I wrote the card', which therefore cannot be true. From F's other statements, we now know that F is Sue and Mel is a truthteller. We know that A is a liar – as A claims, 'Mel lies', which is also claimed by F, a liar – thus, A is not Paul. We know that C must be a liar, as C claims, 'My name is Sue', but F is Sue. Thus we know that Simon (whoever Simon is) is a liar. E claims, 'Mel never lies', which must be true as it contradicts lying A and F; this means that E is correct in claiming that Paul is the author. D must be a liar, as 'Mel and Sue can't write' contradicts truthful E, meaning that D is Simon. Thus, C must be Paul. Paul cannot be A, as A (a liar) falsely claims to be Paul; Paul cannot be B, as B is a truthteller and we know that the author is a liar (and B must be Mel, as B and C are the only ones that don't refer to Mel in the third person and C is a liar where Mel has been identified as a truthteller); Paul cannot be D, as D has already been identified as Simon; Paul cannot be E, as E is both a truthteller and refers to Paul in the third person; and Paul cannot be F, who has already been identified as Sue.]

# WINTERLUDE 4

1. Begin
2. Elbow
3. Ulcer
4. Bowel
5. Binge
6. Serve
7. Paltry
8. Plates
9. Cruel
10. Listen
11. Raptly (or 10 can be 'Raptly' and 11 'Listen')
12. Verse
13. Below
14. Hater
15. Being
16. Partly
17. Enlist
18. Sever
19. Tinsel
20. Petals
21. Staple
22. Lucre
23. Heart
24. Earth

# THE GROD WHO OBLITERATED CHRISTMAS

**Round 1**

1. Yogi [Berra]
2. Fare
3. Interest [*Person of Interest*]
4. Werther [*The Sorrows of Young Werther*; Werther's Originals, originally from the town of Werther in North Rhine-Westphalia]
5. Of [*Of Mice and Men*; *Of Human Bondage*]
6. Format
7. Sow

**Find the place on the map where your gifts are located – Your holiday frolics may not be frustrated!**

Your gifts are in the forest where the froffer-fum plants grow

[Insert *URTSHFOHEFFUPLNGR*, the first letters of each line on the previous page, into these seven answers.]

**Round 2**

1. Maracanã (Ma, Mara, Maraca. . . [adding two letters each time])
2. Tear (Anagrams of metric prefixes: Kilo, Mega, Giga, Tera)
3. Baby (Hasta, La, Vista. . .)
4. EMI (Eminem, Emine [Erdoğan], Emin. . .)
5. Mother (Bitch, Lover, Child. . . [from Meredith Brooks's song 'Bitch'])
6. Al Gore (Sassoon Eskell, Vidal Sassoon,* Gore Vidal. . .)

* In *Rosemary's Baby* (both the novel and the film), Rosemary describes her new haircut as 'It's Vidal Sassoon and it's very in.' To promote the film, Paramount staged a photo shoot of Vidal Sassoon trimming Mia Farrow's hair, which was already short at the time.

7. Parking lot (Swinging hot spot, Boutique, Pink hotel. . . [attractions in paved Paradise, moving backwards, in Joni Mitchell's 'Big Yellow Taxi'])

8. Cloves (Claves, Cleves, Clives. . .)

**Are you out of the maze? Is your brain overloaded?**
**Tell me the message that you have decoded.**

In two packages ele-floots are skulking [Inn, Tupac, Kid, Gisele [Bündchen], Flute, Tsar, Skull, King]

### Round 3

1. Cordelia
2. Ernie [Banks, Irvan and Els]
3. Timon
4. Helen [Mirren and Keller]
5. Esther [Rantzen]
6. Rylan [Clark; Mark Rylance]
7. Carrie [Fisher and White]
8. Vespa [in *Spaceballs*]
9. Ingrid
10. Sandy [Denny]
11. Hades
12. Bevis
13. Margot [Margaret of Valois, known as Margot; Robbie]
14. Honey [Ryder]
15. Grace [*Will and Grace*]
16. Jared [Kushner]

**Which Venns, if they heeded their lust to unwrap**
**Irresistible gifts, would be caught in my trap?**

Grace and Helen's packages contain ele-floots [of short-t**ailed roc**k crabs; squirrelled insid**e, in re**verse; an**timony**; There were clu**es there** instead; ve**ry lang**uidly; th**eir rac**kets and knives; Yes, he did ha**ve**

233

**spar**e quizzes!; They will spend Christmas Day quizz**ing, rid**dling and puzzling!; Next, add in some space**s and** you've got a clue; And some u**sed a h**igh-speed head-scratching device; The drawings **I've b**ooby-trapped perfectly match; cryp**togram**s; Then the Grod took his megap**hone. 'Y**oo-hoo! There's news!'; Will sound out, in or**der, a j**udicious message]

### Round 4

I. Speed
II. Numan
III. Taurus
IV. Chickering
V. Grand
VI. Player [*Ready Player One*]

**So those are the questions – you've had time to read 'em.**
**What is the island that leads you to freedom?**

Rhodes

[The layout of Vennburg is a giant Venn diagram, the Roman numerals on the buildings matching the question numbers in this round. VI, I and II are surnames of famous men named Gary; II, III and IV begin with letters of the Greek alphabet; IV, V and VI may precede 'piano' (Chickering & Sons was a major piano manufacturer based in Boston, Massachusetts). Rhodes fits all three categories.]

# WINTERLUDE 5

1.  *This Is England*
2.  Tomorrow is another day
3.  *Where's Wally?*
4.  'Where Is the Love?'
5.  Brevity is the soul of wit
6.  *Orange Is the New Black*
7.  *O Brother, Where Art Thou?*
8.  *The Only Way Is Essex*

# SHERBERT HICKS
# AND THE BLUE GARFUNKEL

**Round 1**

1. Toreador [popularized by *Carmen*]
2. Mendicant
3. Lighthouse keeper
4. Surgeon
5. Thatcher
6. Chemist
7. Carpenter
8. Quarterback
9. Laundress
10. Warden
11. Weaver
12. Sheriff [Bob Marley being the man in question]
13. Deputy
14. Law enforcement officer
15. Ambassador [by Hans Holbein and Henry James]
16. Animator
17. Mayor

**Who left the note?**

Quentin Plibb

The unaccounted-for words in the note can be rearranged into 'Behave Yourself'; the newspaper reveals that Plibb is the proprietor of 'Behave Yourself!' nightclub.

*F Y I : ENTER EN DEN. PUT CEMENT ART ON MAT OR BACK OF DE – ICER. MEND LIGHT THAT MAY SURGE. UNDRESS. CAN'T CARP OR **BE** SAD AS MIST; AVER (OR RIFF), 'LA, LA! CHER? ER. . . I AM SHE, AN **ELF!**' OR WE **HAVE** WAR. **YOURS**, QU.*

## Round 2

1. John Quincy Adams
2. 'Someone Like You'
3. 'Like Water for Chocolate'
4. Marie Curie
5. Condoleezza Rice
6. *Crème de la Crème*
7. Monica Seles

**To which building is the sculpture being taken?**

Wychwood Manor

[Each answer shares its initials with a location the driver goes past when leaving the En Den: J. Quence's Address (a reference to Jas Quence, mentioned in the newspaper); Silver Linings Yd.; Loon Warehouse, Flt. C; Myers Cres.; Crux Rd.; Co. Durham Lower Course; Mme. Sin's. Each of these contains an abbreviation, and the missing letters (jAS yARd flAt cresCENT rOAd coUNTY mADAme) spell out 'A Saracen to Aunty Ada' (which refers to the 'mediaeval Arab' among the plaster sculptures, which was not mentioned in the list). One can deduce from comparing the reference in the list to 'cousin QW at Axel House' to the newspaper that 'Aunty Ada' is his mother, Ada Wills, whose missing spanner was returned by Hicks. At the very beginning of the quiz, Hicks refers to 'the missing spanner of Wychwood Manor'.]

## Round 3

Serum 2: Overseas [British Overseas Territory]

Serum 3: Right of reply

Serum 4: Below zero

['Overseas' means that you must find words which appear immediately above the names of seas. 'Right of reply' means that you must find words which appear immediately to the right of synonyms for 'reply'. 'Below zero' means that you must find words which appear immediately below synonyms for 'zero'.]

**What is the hidden message describing the effect of Serum 2?**

Place (above Coral) O (above Red) Half (above North) Way (above Labrador) In (above Black) Associate (above Sargasso)

**What is the hidden message describing the effect of Serum 3?**

Disregard (right of Retort) S (right of Riposte) At (right of Counter) The (right of Respond) Start (right of Rejoin) of (right of Answer) Words (right of Reciprocate)

**What is the hidden message describing the effect of Serum 4?**

Disregard (below Nada) Words (below Love) Starting (below Nothing) With (below Scratch) Letters (below Zip) In (below Naught) The (below Nix) Latter (below Duck) Half (below Null) Of (below Void) The (below Nil) Alphabet (below Zilch)

**Which building must you head for now?**

Xeno Glamour

Steps of the plan to find the Blue Simon:

A. GIVING MASSES IS A CERTAIN INDIVIDUAL'S JOB – FIND HIM leads you to *Ovid*. [Ovid is the priest who advertises his services in the newspaper.]

B. FIND HICKS DRAWING LOTS leads you to *Ixodes Cafe* [Bilbert Wickles says that the Ixodes Cafe is full of 'country bumpkins who can't decide the simplest thing except by picking bits of paper at random'.]

C. OVOID leads you to *Toon Format*

D. *Xerxes* [the gifted fencer]

E. XEROXES leads to *Fathom Inc.* [Fathom Inc. is where Hicks has reproductions of the leaflet from the job centre made.]

F. I IGNORE PRESENTS ICILY – WHERE? FIND THE ROAD ON THE HICKS DRAWING PORTRAYING LOTS OF THOROUGHFARES WITHIN THE TOWN leads to *East Oxford Drive* [This is where Professor Marachi coldly ignored Hicks's offer of gifts.]

PROFICIENT WORDPLAY GIVING RISE TO MASSES OF LAUGHTER IS A CERTAIN INDIVIDUAL'S JOB – FIND HIM leads you to *Nightmog* [the professional punster]

H. *Cuccia Expressway*

Taking the first, second, third letter (etc.) from Ovid, Ixodes Cafe, Toon Format, etc., gives you OXOXOXOX. Each location is found in a different square on the map, as the game that Hicks envisages is a giant game of noughts and crosses. The winning move that must be played features 'O' as its ninth letter and should be found in the square on the bottom right of the map. Hence, the Blue Simon is in Xeno Glamour.

**Fill in the blanks**

1. *Connect; I* [US states with the last four letters missing, in alphabetical order]
2. *Dots; In* [words immediately following 'Polka', 'Polk', 'Pol', 'Po' and 'P' in the note]
3. *Over; Present* [follow or precede 'do', 're', 'mi', 'fa', 'so', 'la', 'ti']
4. *Letter; Order* [follow the colours of the rainbow in order: red, orange, yellow, green, blue, indigo, violet]

**In which container are the sculpted Simon and Garfunkel?**

The bag

[Each section of the list which names an item and describes its destination contains the name of a gift given in the song 'The Twelve Days of Christmas'. Each section contains a single letter *i*. If you connect the dots above the letter *i* in the order in which the sections' gifts were given in the song, it forms an arrow pointing at the word 'bag'.]

# WINTERLUDE 6

1. Jed [Stone; Maxwell; Gerald 'Jed' Mercurio]
2. Circular [Circular letter; North Circular and South Circular Roads]
3. MP [Michael Portillo]
4. Amid [Amidst; Pyramid]
5. Kingdom
6. Plain
7. Cave [Nick Cave; *Cave canem* ('Beware of the dog')]
8. 'I Saw Three Ships Come Sailing In'

# THE GIFT ON THE THIRTEENTH DAY

**Round 1**

1. Primrose
2. Rosemary [*Rosemary's Baby*; *Parsley, Sage, Rosemary and Thyme*]
3. Maryland [Baltimore Orioles]
4. Landlady [*Electric Landlady*]
5. Lady Bird [Lady Bird Johnson]
6. Calluses [Sulla]

**Round 2**

1. Titanium
2. Mr Amis [Martin Amis]
3. Oxygen
4. Lato [Grzegorz Lato, in a list of FIFA World Cup Golden Boot winners]
5. Xenon
6. Cartagena
7. Porters
8. Hello ['Hello, gorgeous'; 'Say "hello" to my little friend'; 'You had me at "hello"']

**Round 3**

1. Friand ['Ami' in Mr Amis]
2. Aries
3. Lay
4. Cali
5. Of [*Of Gods and Men*/Of Monsters and Men/*Of Mice and Men*]
6. Neon
7. Emasculator [ASC (American Society of Cinematographers) in 'Emulator']
8. Rome

## Round 4

1. Perles [Shimon Peres]
2. Vin [Vin Diesel; St Vincent]
3. Om
4. Passenger
5. GR [Gioachino Rossini; Alt and AltGr]
6. Mas [Mas Oyama; Mas Que Nada; Grandmaster]
7. Uncan [*Nunca más* is Spanish for 'nevermore']
8. Por ['Por una cabeza' by Carlos Gardel and Alfredo Le Pera; Porny and uncanny]

## Round 5

1. Forge [Corden plays Smithy in *Gavin and Stacey*]
2. Mormon [*The Book of Mormon*]
3. Ivy [Poison Ivy]
4. Algernon [Algernon Sidney; Algernon Swinburne; Algernon Blackwood; *Flowers for Algernon* by Daniel Keyes; Algernon Moncrieff in Oscar Wilde's *The Importance of Being Earnest*]
5. Ex [*Deus ex machina*]
6. Reg [Reg Keys; Reg Varney; Elton John, formerly Reg Dwight]
7. Nessa [Barrett; Nessa and Smithy become parents in *Gavin and Stacey*]
8. Propenol [*A Modest Proposal*; *Indecent Proposal*; Brian Eno]

## Driving out the demons

1. Call Lady Mary prim [Remove 'rose', 'land', 'bird', and 'uses'.]
2. Birdcall [In Round 1, the last four letters of one answer are the first four of the next, with the exception of 'Lady Bird'/'Calluses'.]
3. Halloween [Round 1, which contains 'A' 'E' 'I' and 'U' as separate words, also contains 'Hell', 'Hill', 'Holl' and 'Hull', 'Awe', 'Ewe', 'Iwe' and 'Uwe' and 'An', 'In', 'On' and 'Un'.]
4. Muhammad Ali [Lay, Cali]; George Foreman [Forge Mormon]
5. Falconer

6. Forgiveness [Forge, Ivy, Ex, Nessa]

7. Fairyland [An anagram of 'Friand lay'; Aries rhymes with fairies]

8. Bandicoot [Cali**BAN D**uncan Per**IC**les Rome**O OT**hello]

9. Executioner [Emasculator minus Mas and Lato, plus Xe, Ti, O, Ne]

10. Andy Warhol [Propenol and Algernon share the letters 'loner'; when 'loner' is removed, it leaves the letters 'Pop'. Iggy Pop sang 'The Passenger'. 'Art' is shared in Cartagena and Martin Amis.]

11. Forty Canaries [IV times X; Uncan; Aries]

12. Lone [All of Round 5's answers, when taken as a single string of letters and spelt backwards, are other answers in this quiz – except 'Lone', the last four letters of Propenol spelt backwards.]

13. Group 1: Call Lady Mary Prim, Birdcall, Halloween; 2: Forgiveness, Muhammad Ali; George Foreman, Forty canaries; 3: Executioner, Falconer, Lone; 4: Fairyland, Bandicoot, Andy Warhol [contain 'All', 'For', 'One', 'And']

14. Mercenaries [**Mr** Amis instead of Aramis; Port**ER**s instead of Porthos; Cartag**ENA** instead of D'Artagnan; **ARIE**s instead of Athos; Perles before Vin leads you to pearls before wine; it needs an *s* to make 'pearls before swine'.]

# WINTERLUDE 7

1. Winifred [Winifred Atwell, 'Let's Have Another Party'; St Winifred's School Choir, 'There's No One Quite Like Grandma']
2. Rudolf the Red-Nosed Reindeer
3. Ban Ki-Moon
4. Known as (the) Vixen
5. Myrrh
6. Rudyard Kipling
7. *The Muppet Christmas Carol* [Michael Caine was born Maurice Micklewhite; Statler and Waldorf are muppet characters]
8. Oxen [Oxford]

# THE NUT-KRAKEN

**Which item in the playroom moves diagonally down and right?**

Happy Cow

**Which one moves diagonally down and left?**

Batman, Jr.

[The letter can be rephrased as: **H**ave you helped yourself to a bass while partaking in a **b**reak-/**I**n **at** the Palladium during a concert satirizing Glenn Gould? Refine your **a**rtistry! Even/**Y**ou are **p**roficient enough on the piano, my lovely, **t**o play Chop-/Sticks, which may **p**erhaps be seen as too **m**eaningless for an up-/Grade of this nature? **Y**ou'll easily escape shock and **a**mazement if I say, 'Remember!/The fauna of a European **c**ity is more majestic than **n**ew artifices, such as your candle-/Holder of great beauty. One thinks **o**f nature, calmly and jovially. Isn't it awful to rid Bel-/Fast of fish? I know that you **w**ere **r**eportedly planning to do such a thing soon.']

**ACROSS:**

A. Upset
B. May not
C. Informal local
D. Lychees [mainly cheese]
E. Ire
F. *It*
G. Many make
H. Atmometer
I. Eucalyptus
J. BSE [an 'orphan initialism' which originally stood for Bombay Stock Exchange; Bovine Spongiform Encephalopathy]
K. Jura
L. Men [*Men in Black* and *No Country for Old Men*]
M. Loren [Sophia Loren, who won an Oscar for her performance in the 1960 film *Two Women*]
N. Newsstand
O. Take urns

P. Shred

Q. Ro [Ro Laren; Romania]

**DOWN:**

A. Tuscany [Florence Nightingale, born in Florence]

B. Marsh light [Ngaio Marsh]

C. Flak

D. Site

E. Moi [Daniel arap Moi]

F. Era

G. Moves ramp

H. Ton

I. Cometh [Cometh the hour, cometh the man/*The Iceman Cometh*]

J. Jumble sale

K. Dor [Ballon d'Or and Palme d'Or]

L. Sons [Sons of Kemet/*Sons and Lovers*/*Sons of Anarchy*]

M. Er [Erbium, one of four elements discovered in (and named after) Ytterby]

N. Do

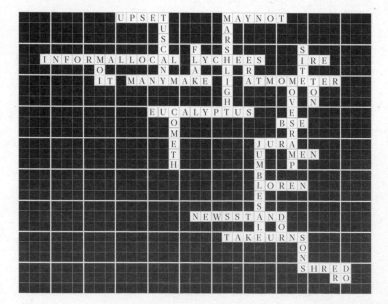

**ACROSS:**

2. Lyre

5. Trencherman [Herman Melville and Herman Wouk in *Moby-Dick* and *The Caine Mutiny* respectively]

7. Euchre

8. Tara [Browne and Palmer-Tomkinson]

9. Mater [Alma; Stabat]

11. Me [Maine]

12. Some [*Some Mothers Do 'Ave 'Em*; *Some Like It Hot*]

13. Loo

17. Et

19. Jut

20. Tan [Amy and Shaun]

21. Ned [Edward 'Ned' Leeds, Eddard 'Ned' Stark and Nedward 'Ned' Flanders]

25. Italy

**DOWN:**

3. Sitcom

4. Ether [Esther]

6. Mo

10. Tondo

15. Ert [Estrogen replacement therapy]

16. Salt [Salt of the earth; Worth one's salt; Rub salt into the wound; Take with a pinch (or grain) of salt]

18. Tusk [Donald and Elon (voiced by Elon Musk)]

22. DOS (or DoS) [Disk Operating System; Denial of service]

24. Sony [Sonny and sonus]

**What are the four answers in the grid that tell you which pieces you must move and how you must move them?**

Flashlamp moves right; Ibsen follows scales; Marble can jump; Make-up turns at 'make up' synonyms [When the first crossword is divided into 3x3 squares, they can be rearranged (without rotation) into the second crossword, so that blank entries can be filled using the remaining squares from the first grid.]

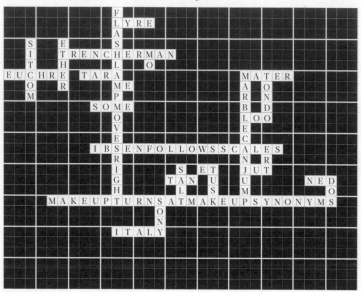

**What is the final message, which tells you what to move and how, so that the wicked creature's muddles and messes can be undone forever?**

'Move apes horizontally' [In Dieselmotor's letter, find strings of letters of the same length as the number of the grid references where the moving items coincide, which occur between two instances of the same letter found in the grid references. 'M' appears between two of the letter *l* in 'calmly' (the make-up bag and flashlamp coincide on l1); 'ove' appears between two of the letter *l* in 'lovely' (the marble and happy cow coincide on l3); 'apesho' appears between two of the letter *c* in 'escape shock' (the flashlamp and Batman, Jr. coincide on c6); 'riz' appears between two of the letter *i* in 'satirizing' (Ibsen and the marble coincide on i3); 'ont' appears between two of the letter *h* in 'enough on the' (Ibsen and the marble also coincide on h3); 'ally' appears between two of the letter *i* in 'jovially. Isn't' (the make-up bag and Ibsen coincide on i4).]

# WINTERLUDE 8

1. De
2. Tart
3. Surf's up
4. Mark Ruffalo
5. Olaf
6. Fur [Darfur]
7. Krampus
8. Frustrated

# THE CROW MAN

## Joining the letters and numbers in the book

IV; K9; TP; 4C [Homophones of 'ivy', 'canine', 'tepee' and 'foresee', which are indicated by the book's symbols]

## The magic word

Horrify [Take the only letter of the alphabet missing from each line]

## The map

1i is the location of the crows' party [The tick is in the lower case; 1i is the only square containing lowercase letters]

## The crows' mysterious diagram

Anus; Onus [The chief crow is showing a word ladder with two entries missing: Ants, _____, _____, Ones, Ores, Oreo, Orzo, Ouzo. Beneath it, the footprints represent different letters used in the word ladder]

## The war

1974 Turkish invasion of Cyprus [An anagram of the previous answers, plus S7, which was seen on the sole of the crop-trampler's boot]

# WINTERLUDE 9

1. Keeping the 'term' in Easter Monday
2. Keeping the 'posited' in Opposite Day
3. Keeping the 'alms' in Palm Sunday
4. Keeping the 'wind' in Darwin Day
5. Keeping the 'dig' in Mardi Gras
6. Keeping the 'arse' in New Year's Eve
7. Keeping the 'ankh' in a bank holiday
8. Keeping the 'allow' in Halloween

# THE BOY WHO LIVED BY HIMSELF

**Genghis's poem**

1. *Swingers* (wasp's wing, ersatz)
2. *Orlando* (whorl/And oafish)
3. *Casino* (son, is acidic)
4. *Crash* (with sarcasm) [This refers to David Cronenberg's *Crash* rather than its Paul Haggis-directed, Best Picture-winning namesake.]
5. *Magnolia* ([samurai] long, amusing)
6. *Singles* (amusing lessons)
7. *Lone Star* (clones tarantulas)
8. *Rushmore* (toothbrush/Moreover)
9. *Fargo* (taboo graffiti)
10. *Titanic* (ricin!'/'A titch)
11. *Heat* (flesh-eating)
12. *Seven* (ants!/Even)
13. *Naked* (snake deep)
14. *JFK* (dank fjord)
15. *Audition* (applaud it/I only)
16. *The Matrix* (anthem/A Trixie)

**The steps**

1. Magnesium
2. Victoriana
3. Cannonball
4. Enoch Powell
5. Moustache (Walrus/Pencil/Toothbrush)
6. Tsarevna (Dzhokhar and Tamerlan Tsarnaev)
7. Misnomer
8. Acrostic
9. Shevchenko (Valentina/Taras/Andriy)
10. Leon (Leon Czolgosz/Donna Leon/Kings of Leon)

**Which two steps will harmlessly turn the TV on and off?**

Steps 2 and 5 are safe, as they will do nothing more than switch on the TV. (The words MICE, CANS, TV, CANS, CANS, TV, MICE can be found horizontally in the grid, forming a staircase pattern.)

**Now, what's my secret, boys?**

'Killer'.

(As Question 8 suggests, the introduction forms an acrostic. The first letters of each sentence read, 'Remove words on steps'. Genghis has stated that his hero is the central character of *Home Alone*, Kevin McCallister. When the letters of 'MICE CANS TV' are removed from 'KEVIN MCCALLISTER', you are left with the word 'KILLER'. Genghis is a murderer.)

**The spare room and the mantelpiece**

1. Nuclear
2. *Speed*
3. Roll
4. Blue
5. Phoenix
6. Bell (Kristen and Jamie)
7. Silence ('The rest is silence' and 'The Sound of Silence')

**In what order do you arrange them?**

From left to right: 1. Family 2. Envelope 3. Power 4. Belt 5. Barrel 6. Toilet 7. California 8. Carey (the mask depicts Carey Mulligan) 9. River 10. Rain 11. Liberty 12. Division 13. Dumb 14. Hymn 15. Tarot

(1, 2, and 3 may follow 'nuclear' to make phrases; 3, 4 and 5 are verbs synonymous with 'speed'; 5, 6 and 7 may precede 'roll' to make phrases; 7, 8 and 9 are tracks from Joni Mitchell's album *Blue*; 9, 10 and 11 are forenames of Phoenix siblings; 11, 12 and 13 may precede 'bell' to make phrases; and 13, 14 and 15 end in silent letters.)

## What number do you dial?

The number that you dial is 3209. ('Agnes', 'she', 'echo' and 'male' can all be found in the grid.)

With Agnes Reed's body having been discovered last night, police warned that she wouldn't be the last of the South Bend Shovel Slayer's victims. Bystanders heard the screech, "I'll be your pulverizer!" echo ominously through the alley and, rushing towards the murder scene, witnessed the culprit – young, thin, male – inelegantly running away.

## Which pizza do you order?

Four Seasons

['Winter' could replace 'envelope' (as both follow 'nuclear'). 'Spring' could replace 'toilet' (as both precede 'roll'). 'Summer' could replace 'Rain' (as both are forenames of Phoenix siblings). 'Autumn' could replace 'hymn' (as both end in silent letters). So you must order a Four Seasons pizza.]

## You type a password. What do you type?

The password is 'Christmas' (the fifth letter of 'Artichoke', the first letter of 'ham', etc.)

## The dining room

1. Crack
2. Next
3. Round
4. By
5. Acting
6. Like
7. Unbelievable (*The Unbelievable Truth*)
8. Rebecca

## The basement

1. G (Kenny, Warren and Gina)
2. Joe (the sandwich and action figure being Sloppy Joe and G.I. Joe respectively)
3. MP (melting point, mezzo piano, Member of Parliament)
4. Pub
5. NPO (Nil per os and non-profit organization)
6. HS (Hailee Steinfeld, Harry Styles and Harold Shipman)
7. Pet (Pet Shop Boys, *Auf Wiedersehen, Pet* and *Pet Sematary*)
8. CP (Colin Powell, Charlie Parker and Chris Pratt)
9. Oft

## In which grid reference do you find the Von Millicent fortune?

f2

[To find the Von Millicent fortune, follow the advice in the dining room's questions and 'act like unbelievable Rebecca'. This refers to the line from Genghis's poem: 'I can't believe she [Rebecca] reduced the bout to ants!' To reduce 'bout' to 'ants', you move each letter one place back in alphabetical order. If you do the same to the answers in the final round, you are left with the string of letters 'FINDLOOTAMONGRODSBONES'. To identify which bones belong to Rod, bear in mind that Genghis's poem accuses Rod of stealing his toothbrush, indicating that the figure wearing glasses and a cap in the photo must be Rod, as he is holding Genghis's toothbrush. The fortune is in f2.]

## In which grid reference do you find the only safe exit?

a2

[To find the safe escape route, follow the Reverend's advice: 'To find the path to salvation, start from scratch.' Start from where Merv is scratching himself and continue in the direction of each arrow you come across; they lead you to the manhole cover shown in a2.]

# WINTERLUDE 10

1. Contain names of Chinese dynasties with an *s* added at the end [Hans (Gruber); (Je) Suis (Charlie); Songs [*of Innocence and Experience*]; (Tyrone) Mings]

2. Can precede 'Day' to make U2 songs

3. Follow 'Santa' to make cities in California [Barbara; Cruz; Monica; Ana (de Armas)]

4. Injuries suffered by the Wet Bandits in *Home Alone*

5. 'Closed' pairs of rhyming words (that is, pairs of words that no other English word rhymes with)

6. Known by a single initial followed by a surname: O. Henry; M. Bison; J. Mascis; E. Nesbit

7. Have brothers named George [George Bailey being the protagonist of *It's a Wonderful Life*]

8. Feature cameos by Donald Trump

# GOOD QUEEN WESSELSBRON

1A. Sickle

1B. Depicting

2A. Submersible [an anagram of 'Blurb', 'Seem', 'Is']

2B. Snow

3A. Impact

3B. By stealth [the National Health Service]

4A. 'Reet Petite'

4B. Edged

5A. 'Blurred Lines'

5B. Red

6A. FIFPro

6B. Coenzymes

7A. Severn [Dan Severn]

7B. Newcastle

8A. Solicitor

8B. Throat [Inuit and Tuvan throat singing]

9A. Not found [a reference to the '404 Not Found' status code]

9B. Capital

10A. Howerd [Frankie Howerd]

10B. Sgt. Pepper

11A. Stonewall

11B. Go fast

12A. Anarchiste [Catharine's]

12B. Cover

13A. End [*The Low End Theory*; *At World's End*; Preston North End]

13B. Blockbusters

### The meeting place

The submerged castle of Astana [The voice is telling you 'Think of three words used when depicting snow'. These are (in keeping with this quiz's theme) 'deep', 'crisp' and 'even'. *Deep* precedes *Impact*, *Red*, *Throat*, *Cover* and *End* to make film titles; above these five answers are SUBMER GED CASTLE OFAST ANA.]

### The game

Connect Four ['GOLDEN WONDER', 'CHEETOS', 'DORITOS', 'KETTLE CHIPS' and 'PRINGLES' are found diagonally, creating pockets of letters which spell out 'CONNECT FOUR'.]

### The creature's identity

A red lion

(The seven six-letter answers are Sickle, Impact, FIFPro, Severn, Throat, Howerd and Go Fast. You must take their even letters [applying 'even', the final adjective referring to snow] to make Ike, Mat, IPO, E'en, Hot, OED and Oat. These, respectively, can be defined by the following trios of words found within the questions: White House resident; where cat sat; initial public offering; shortening of even; 'spicy', 'fiery', 'attractive'; *Oxford English Dictionary*; very common cereal. If the second words of each trio are arranged in the order in which they occur in the questions, they spell out 'Fiery cat of common English public house'; The Red Lion is among England's most common pub names.)

# WINTERLUDE 11

1. Cricket [The Talking Cricket in *Pinocchio*, reimagined as Jiminy Cricket]
2. Sheldon Leonard [*The Big Bang Theory* being the sitcom]
3. 'Jingle Bells'
4. Tony the Tiger
5. They are named after patients rather than doctors.
6. 'In the Bleak Midwinter' [Beth (Tweddle), D, *A Wrinkle in Time*]
7. Ferdinand [von Zeppelin; Porsche; Magellan]
8. *Elf* and *Once* ['Eleven' in German and Spanish]

# DIE, HARDLY

**Round 1**

1. Albuquerque
2. Destiny
3. Ayrton Senna
4. *The Confirmation*
5. Rage Against the Machine
6. *Shrek*
7. Fireworks
8. Swordsman

**Round 2**

1. Generation
2. Swiss [Swiss army knife; Swiss Re; *Swiss Family Robinson*]
3. Caller
4. Boney
5. Either [Wolfgang Reitherman]
6. Grand [*Grand Ole Opry*, Grand National, *Grand Theft Auto*]
7. Kit [Carson; Harington]

**What does the terrorist plan to harness, in order to unleash it and destroy the world?**

Latent heat [Til implies, when she says, 'Get to the heart of every answer', that you must take the middle three letters of every answer; these spell out 'Questions' first three words'. Take the first three words of every question to spell out three further questions: Which city is the building in? The event is occurring on what day of the month of May? Comer means to what in Spanish? The first answer is LA (Los Angeles, which is also the setting for *Die Hard*). The second answer can be deduced from the introduction, the calendar and the guardroom: the Juggle-O-Matic has been installed (so it's on or after 7 May) and is working (so it's not a weekend), but the leak has not yet been fixed (so it's before 13 May), and it's not Tuesday or Wednesday (as Til has never missed one of Lani's classes on those evenings) or Friday (as we know from the driver at the beginning), so the event occurs on the tenth. *Comer* means 'to eat' in Spanish. LA + tenth + eat = latent heat.]

**What is the hidden message of Round 2, which will help you work out the terrorist's identity?**

Take Lani from display [Different words may follow the answers in Round 2 so that they match the books in Til's pile: Generation *Y*, Swiss *Alps*, Caller *ID*, Boney *M*, Either/*Or* (a work by Søren Kierkegaard), Grand *Finale*, Kit*Kat*. Spell *Y ALPS ID M OR FINALE KAT* backwards for the hidden message.]

**Who is the terrorist?**

Psi Veldt ['Take Lani from display' means that you should remove the road markings on Lani's poster from the display, so that 'OBEBABE' now resembles the word 'COLONEL'. This would appear to point to Gerald Smitz – however, the calendar tells us that the computer has not yet been fixed and uses *L* where *R* is meant. This points us to the *coroner*, Psi Veldt.]

### Round 3

1. Paganism [Paganini]
2. Songbirds
3. Incombustible
4. Encase [Seneca/Seance]
5. Caesium [Cesium]
6. House martin [Martin Lawrence; *Big Momma's House*]
7. Step [In Alcoholics Anonymous' twelve-step programme]

**What is the hidden message of this round, which instigates an uproar among the hostages?**

Henry wears proof she cheats on Heath [Use the instructions to get *heathenry*, *wheatears*, *heatproof*, *sheathe*, *Cs*, *Heaton* (Paul Heaton from the Housemartins), *H* (from Steps) from this round. Remove and add 'heat' as appropriate to reveal that Henry's heart necklace was a token of love from Psi.]

## Round 4

1. Thicken
2. Witness
3. Clicked
4. At first [*Love at First Sting*; *Love at First Bite*; *Married at First Sight*]
5. Missive [Per-; Dis-; Sub-]
6. Maracas [Mascara]

### What is the four-digit combination?

1036

[The answers to Round 3 must be entered into a grid as depicted in the room containing the 'Obe Babe'. The propellor contains the letters CLU HAT, such that the propellor can be moved into a different position to alter the words in the grid. To make WITNESS into WITLESS ('foolish'), it must be vertical (|); to make THICKEN into CHICKEN ('bird'), it must be diagonal (\); to make MARACAS into CARACAS ('capital city'), it must be a mirror image of the previous diagonal (/); and to make MISSIVE into MISLIVE ('lead a bad life'), it must be vertical again (|), such that the four propellor positions can join into the shape of a capital M. THICKET CLUCKED gives you an X (the two propellor positions must be overlaid, as there are no semi-colons); MASSIVE MISSILE and CLICHÉD CHICKEN also give you Xs. MAR A CAT and ATHIRST combine to form a V, and WITLESS again gives you an I. You have made MXXXVI, the Roman numeral for 1036.]

## Round 5

1. The Devil's Path [an anagram of 'Psi Heath Veldt']
2. Aardvarks
3. Seeds [Nick Cave and the Bad Seeds]
4. Illusions
5. Ulnar loop [*Lunar Pool*]
6. Empties
7. Rails

## What is the hidden message?

I have set up this surprise. AVSTI [Decode the message to the left of the safe, using the windows of the building (each of which represents a different letter of the alphabet, starting from A in the top left corner). 'DIRECTION ON ENTRY' reads the text on the top left, beneath which is written 'NORTH', 'EAST', 'SOUTH', 'WEST'. 'FIRST', 'MIDDLE', 'LAST' are written above the ticks. Each answer in Round 5 corresponds to an item in the roof plan; take the path indicated by the Obe Corporation's logo displayed outside the building, taking the first and last letters of the item if moving northwards into it, first and middle letters of the item if moving eastwards into it, etc. Thus, you end up with THE DEVIL'S PATH (east): IH; AARDVARKS (south): AV; SEEDS (east): ES; EMPTIES (south): ET; ULNAR LOOP (north): UP; THE DEVIL'S PATH (north): TH; ILLUSIONS (west): ISS ; ULNAR LOOP (west): URP; RAILS (south): RI; SEEDS (south): SE; AARDVARKS (west): AVS; THE DEVIL'S PATH (south): TI. AVSTI is Anthony Von Saint Tibbins-Ibbs, your ex-husband, who has set up the whole 'terrorist plot' as a ruse to attempt to win you back.]

# WINTERLUDE 12

1. Flambéed: Feed
2. Revealed: Reed
3. Bowlegged: Bowled
4. *Under Milk Wood*: Underwood
5. Polar decomposition: Poe composition
6. Debriefer: Defer
7. Hammock: Mock
8. Seven is one more than six: See more than six

# INTO THE FRIDGE

## SADIE

### The fridge's message

If you say, 'Susan Calman', a concealed entrance opens [This message can be spelt out by rearranging (without anagramming) *If. . . .*, *Once*, *Ys*, *O*, *USA*, *Us*, *Pens*, *Trance*, *Ale*, *ANC*, *Almanac*, *Yo*, *Den*.]

## ERICK

### The thought that worms its way into your head

'Betray your siblings' [Connect up the lines in the stars to find this message enclosed within them.]

### The directions to the castle

Old Moor leads to Mount Donorel. Then go down Good Gert Road. Turn right at Hag's Dwelling. Head west at the Spear to the bush. [You must seek the quickest route from Angel to 'Shepherd's', both of which can precede 'Delight'; the missing letters spell out the directions.]

## THE NOTE

### PEDRO, SADIE, LAKRISHA

Wordsearch:

 Settee (indiscr**eet, tes**tifying)

 Divan (dow**n, avid**ly)

 Ottoman (b**ottom – an**d)

 Cabinet (lis**ten I bac**kflipped)

 Stool (ari**sto, ol**igarch)

 Closet (dis**close t**he)

 Canape (sauc**epan, ac**cused)

265

Alternating letters:

    Parsley (**s**p**e**a**k** **r**a**s**h**l**y. **E**eyore-like)

    Nemean Lion (moo**n**b**e**a**m**, **h**e **w**a**s**n't **l**ai**d** o**n** **n**ormal)

    Cowardly Lion (**s**ci**o**n! **W**ha**t** **r**ud**e** 'l**o**ya**l**' **b**ico**r**n**s**)

    World Cup Willie (**l**a**w**c**o**u**r**t (**l**a**d**s **c**lum**p**, **a**w**a**i**t** **l**i**l**y **i**ce)

    Mufasa (infa**m**o**u**s **f**la**g**st**a**f**f**)

<h2 style="text-align:center">ERICK</h2>

Anagrams:

    Wicked Witch of the West (**with twits [we checked, of]**)

    Baba Yaga (**a gay ABBA**)

    Maleficent (**Face Melt in**)

    Morgan le Fay (**of mangy earl**)

    Hermione Granger (**engorge her arm in**)

    Mildred Hubble (**dumbbell! I herd**)

<h2 style="text-align:center">ALL</h2>

<h2 style="text-align:center">CHAPTER 1: SUSPICIOUS BEAVERS</h2>

1. Hymn ['Hymn for the Weekend'; 'Battle Hymn of the Republic']
2. Lot
3. Hat [*Top Hat*; *The Cat in the Hat*]
4. PEDRO – Three

   SADIE – I [Remember that Sadie replaces numbers with Roman numerals when she answers questions.]

   ERICK – Seven

   LAKRISHA – Two

   [You are looking for palindromes (Stanley Yelnats; Lon Nol; Navan) – the map's palindromic place names are Peelsleep, Epe and E.]

5. PEDRO – Cain

   SADIE – Noah

   ERICK – Abel

   LAKRISHA – Eve

6. PEDRO – Ba [Between the four fenceposts joined together ('near where four stand united') and the rock ('Pedro' is derived from the Greek for 'rock')]

   SADIE – St Clew ['Is' is removed from 'C. S. Lewis' and replaced with 'T' for 'tango' to make an anagram of 'St Clew']

   ERICK – Oar

   LAKRISHA – Berich [The closest place to Clig Fipper (a spoonerism of 'Fig Clipper') as the crow flies]

7. *The Man Who Shot Liberty Valance* [An anagram of previous answers, plus 'Wolves' (for Pedro), 'Beaver' (for Sadie), 'Witch' (for Erick) and 'Aslan' (for Lakrisha)]

## CHAPTER 2: THE DISAPPEARANCE OF ERICK

1. Ach

2. Target

3. Outer Hebrides [Ronay, Barra, Lewis and Harris]

4. Chorus

5. Lace

6. Sting [Gordon Sumner]

7. 'Our House'

**In which direction must Pedro, Sadie, Lakrisha and the Beavers go to find Su Samuru and avoid the Sorceress's minions?**

8. South [The previous seven answers contain the letters *S, O, U, T* and *H* four times each in total.]

## LAKRISHA

**The message of reassurance**

Reach lasting solace [Add the notes of Mr Ringo's tune, as seen on the stave, to the beginnings of 'Ach', 'Sting', 'Lace'.]

**Shading by numbers**

Page 273 [The underlined words can all follow 'prime'; make the page number by adding up prime numbers – enclosed within spaces forming the shape of an axe, which is the weapon for which you exchange your pencil and paper.]

**The message leading to the final object**

Gain a tank [You 'behead' answers by removing their initial letter. If you do this to Chapter 5, Question 6, Chapter 4, Question 6 and Chapter 5, Question 1, you spell out GAINATANK.]

**ALL**

### CHAPTER 3: AT THE SORCERESS'S CASTLE

1. Lie
2. Flavour of quark [*Keeping **Up** with the Kardashians*; System of a **Down**; *Rock **Bottom***; *Jonathan **Strange** and Mr Norrell*]
3. Named after a city in Morocco [Plaça de Tetuan, Tangerine, *Casablanca*]
4. Sinn Féin
5. Home Secretary
6. Ellen MacArthur
7. A *Carry On* film title [*Loving*, (Cressida) Dick, *Girls*, Henry]
8. Jofra Archer
9. a, c, d, g, h, j, k, l [The hat worn by each creature corresponds to a previous answer in this round: Lie = pork-pie; Flavour of quark = top; Named after a city in Morocco = fez; Sinn Féin = party; Home Secretary = [Jack] Straw; Ellen MacArthur = boater; A *Carry On* film title = cowboy; Jofra Archer = bowler.]

**ALL**

### CHAPTER 4: ETHELBERT ATTACKS

1. *N* [*Chip 'n Dale: Rescue Rangers*; Guns N' Roses; 'I Love Rock 'N' Roll']
2. If
3. WTF [Tourism Federation of Wisconsin, formerly the Wisconsin Tourism Federation; *Whiskey Tango Foxtrot*]
4. Yser [Isère]

5. Lento [Nick Nolte; Elton John]

6. Piñata

7. Provoke

8. Atheists

9. a; put it on Ethelbert's skates. [Look at the Pyramid of Fenris on your map. If you insert your answers vertically into the grid and then read them diagonally from right to left as indicated by the arrows on the map, it spells out 'Apply wintriest Fhonne Fev at Rio to skates'. The Fhonne Fev will anchor him, helpless, to the ground.]

**ALL**

## CHAPTER 5: THE ROUT

1. Ink [Rorschach]

2. Long [Night of the Long Knives, Long jump, Luz Long (Jesse Owens, the winner of the long jump at the 1936 Berlin Olympics, described Hitler as 'a man of dignity')]

3. Zinc [Cinzano is an anagram of 'zinc on a']

4. Darwin

5. Link [character in the *Legend of Zelda* games]

6. AGA

7. Stink [*Mr Stink* by David Walliams; Joseph Bazalgette created a London sewer system]

8. Prong

9. Think [*Who Do You Think You Are?*; 'Don't Think Twice, It's Alright']

10. Abracadabra [The 'group which inspired four mice' is ABBA (as seen in Ethelbert's note and Mr Ringo's poster) and the rhyme scheme of the words on the tree stump is ABBA. The rhyme scheme of the first nine questions of this round is ABACADABA; the otter's lost letter – that is, the letter *r*, which is the only one not found in 'Now, be savvy like a fox! Decode the ancient quiz-song! Jump to it!' – must be inserted twice.]

## ERICK

The two questions in the previous round, between which you have sneaked off unnoticed

2 and 3 [Following the Sorceress's earlier advice, find the phrase 'Get out' in 'Target'; 'Outer Hebrides'.]

## SADIE

### The enchantress you impale with your arrow

Helen is her name [Look at the card the Professor gave you. Its dots correspond to questions in the chapters of this quiz. A straight line from (Jofra) *Archer* to *Target* passes through the letters *HELEN*.]

### When to blow your horn

After the answers 'Ink', 'Long', 'Stink' and 'Prong' [These may precede the word 'horn' to make new words – as can 'leg', 'shoe', 'fog' and 'green', which are clued in the poem which accompanies the horn. A stinkhorn is a fungus and a pronghorn is a deer-like North American mammal.]

## PEDRO

### The secret that the wicked conceal

'There is magic deeper than deep magic' [Spelt out by the letters which the wicked animals conceal on the map]

### Su Samuru's anagram

'Provoke' and 'If' [An anagram of 'Prokofiev', the composer of *Peter and the Wolf*]

### How Pedro will be known

King Pedro the Extravagant ['Navy' needs an *extra v* to become 'navvy'. *Aga* is a palindrome. Darwin is the capital of *NT* (Northern Territory, Australia).]

# EPILOGUE

1. Wilma [Rudolph; Mankiller; Flintstone]
2. Refocus ['Rests' divided into *rest/s*]
3. Dolly Parton [Jolene]
4. Nominally [phenomenally]
5. Codenames [a table-top game, with editions including *Pictures*, *Duet* and *Deep Undercover*]
6. James B. Steedman [a reference to the superhero team and TV series sharing the name *The Avengers*]
7. Reconciliation Day
8. Norman [Bates and Osborn, in *Psycho* and *Spider-Man* comics respectively]

**What, according to the mysterious figure, must you not do when answering the question in the grid?**

Err [The dimension which contains the name of another dimension within it is 'The Gift on the Thirteenth Day', which contains 'Into the Fridge'. 'All for one and one for all' can be translated literally into French as *Tous pour un et un pour tous*, where *e* is the only letter in the first half of the alphabet. In 'Abracadabra', the two *r*s are the only letters in the second half of the alphabet.]

**What is the answer to the question in the grid?**

Satan [If you treat all letters in the first half of the alphabet as paths and all the letters in the second half of the alphabet as walls, you spell out (*There is a*) *Cecil B. DeMille film called Madam* (*who?*). Question 7 of Winterlude 11 mentions Cecil B. DeMille's *Madam Satan*.]

**Who is the mysterious figure *really*?**

Santa [Take the first word of each Winterlude to spell out 'You must transport the last letter of your answer to the centre'.]

# ACKNOWLEDGEMENTS

If you've encountered puzzles within this book that make you feel like you're trying to chop down a tree but your axe is made of sponge cake, and you've refrained from destroying this book, I owe you a great debt of gratitude.

Rida Vaquas offers analysis so sharp that it can behead the Statue of Liberty with a single blow. My agent, Luke Ingram, is kind and thoughtful, and any word he speaks is guaranteed to exude wit and compassion. My brilliant editor Cecilia Stein showed a faith in this book I hope I can justify; on the first day we spoke, I knew that Frank and Stein could create something truly monstrous together. David Inglesfield copy-edited the book; to call this labyrinthine text difficult to handle is an understatement, but he devoted a lot of meticulous work to it.

My wonderful, inspiring daughter Eve, full of playfulness and imagination, is five (six by the time this is published), and brings us all joy. My beloved son Lawrie, who is three (four by the time this is published – and four feels like a milestone!), invents quiz questions, including 'Hairbrushes have legs – true or false?' My baby Daphna's deep and radiant smiles knock me for six, and it's a delight and an honour to witness her grow. Masha is so supportive even when my workdays stretch far longer than nine to five; one way or another, I'm determined that I'm going to make it up to her!

# NOTES

# NOTES

# NOTES

# NOTES

# NOTES

# NOTES

# NOTES